GILL'S IRISH LIVES

THEOBALD
WOLFE TONE

HENRY BOYLAN

GILL AND MACMILLAN

First published 1981 by
Gill and Macmillan Ltd
Goldenbridge
Dublin 8
with associated companies in
London, New York, Delhi, Hong Kong,
Johannesburg, Lagos, Melbourne,
Singapore, Tokyo

available in this series:
Michael Collins (Leon Ó Broin)
Sean O'Casey (Hugh Hunt)
C. S. Parnell (Paul Bew)
James Craig (Patrick Buckland)
James Joyce (Peter Costello)
Eamon de Valera (T. Ryle Dwyer)
Daniel O'Connell (Fergus O'Ferrall)
Theobald Wolfe Tone (Henry Boylan)
Edward Carson (A. T. Q. Stewart)
James Connolly (Ruth Dudley Edwards)
Arthur Griffith (Calton Younger)

Origination by Healyset, Dublin
Printed and bound in Great Britain by
Redwood Burn Ltd., Trowbridge, Wiltshire.

Contents

1. Early Life, Marriage and London   1

2. Dublin, the Irish Bar and the United Irishmen   12

3. The Catholic Committee   25

4. The Jackson Affair and Exile to America   41

5. Mission in France   62

6. Bantry Bay   86

7. An Officer in the French Army   107

8. Homecoming   126

References   138

Select Bibliography   140

Index   143

Note on References

Except where indicated by a specific footnote reference, all quotations from Tone's writings are taken
from an edition of his autobiography prepared by his
son, William, and published in two volumes in Washington D.C. in 1826.

1
Early Life, Marriage and London

Theobald Wolfe Tone was born on 20 June 1763 at 44 Stafford Street (now Wolfe Tone Street), Dublin.

George III of Great Britain and Ireland had begun his sixty-year reign three years earlier. Before Tone died by his own hand in the Provost's Prison in Dublin on 19 November 1798, the American colonies had revolted; Thomas Paine had published his radical *Rights of Man,* of which 200,000 copies were sold; Revolutionary France had guillotined her 'moral' monarch, Louis XVI, and his queen, Marie Antoinette; 'Grattan's Parliament', so-called, had begun its brief life; and Tone himself had twice sailed to the Irish shore through wintry gales with French expeditions, in high hopes of 'breaking the connection with England'.

Tone's background and education in no way foreshadowed his romantic and tragic life. His father, Peter Tone, was a coachmaker and the son of a prosperous freehold tenant on the estate of the Wolfes of Blackhall, near Clane, in Co. Kildare. He called his first-born after the young squire, Theobald Wolfe. There was a double connection with the family, for Peter's wife, Margaret, lived in the Wolfe mansion before her marriage, as a companion to Mrs Wolfe.

Margaret was the daughter of a sea captain in the East India trade, called Lamport, who came from Drogheda. Neither Peter nor Margaret Tone appear to have been in any way remarkable, but every one

of their five children who survived childhood had, as
Theobald put it, 'a wild spirit of adventure'. William, the second child, born in 1764, saw service with the East India Company on the island of St Helena and later in India, and was killed in the Mahratta War of 1802. Matthew came next in 1771, and after seeking his fortune in America and the West Indies, joined the French army and landed at Killala with Humbert in August 1798. He was captured, court-martialled and hanged. The only daughter, Mary, born in 1774, was as spirited as her brothers, and accompanied Theobald on his exile to America in 1795. On the return passage, she and a fellow-passenger, a young Swiss merchant named Giauque, fell in love. They were married in Hamburg. She too, died young, in the French colony of San Domingo, whether in an epidemic or a massacre is not certain. The youngest, Arthur, born in 1782, sailed for the East Indies at the age of eighteen as an officer in the Dutch navy and was never heard of again.

At eight or nine years, Theobald was sent to a good preparatory school where he showed such exceptional talent that the master, Sisson Darling, recommended to his father that he should be sent to a secondary or classical school and prepared for Trinity College, with the prospect of there winning a fellowship. Accordingly, he was entered at the school of a clergyman named Craig, in Stafford Street, near to his home. When he was about fifteen, his father failed in business and went back to live on some land he had inherited near Bodenstown in Co. Kildare, leaving young Theobald in lodgings with friends.

Craig was clearly no disciplinarian, for Theobald pleased himself as to when he attended lessons, and with other idle boys, spent half the day on country walks or bathing in the sea, or, their favourite past-time, watching military parades in the Phoenix Park.

At that early age he was seized, he said, with 'an untamable desire to become a soldier'. The prospect of entering the university filled him with horror and disgust and in his own words, 'I thought that an ensign in a marching regiment was the happiest creature living. Besides, being approaching seventeen years of age, woman began to appear lovely in my eyes and I very wisely thought that a red coat and cockade with a pair of gold epaulettes would aid me considerably in my approaches to the objects of my adoration.' Craig became alarmed lest he should be blamed for Tone's probable failure at the entrance examination to Trinity, and belatedly told Peter Tone of his son's idleness. Tone senior would not hear of any change of plan and with a bad grace Theobald set to serious study. His quick mind made up for his previous neglect and he entered Trinity College in February 1781, some months before reaching eighteen.

Tone grew to manhood as his native city increased in size and wealth. Eighteenth-century Dublin could boast of public buildings as impressive as visiting notables had seen elsewhere in Europe. The Irish Parliament House in College Green, with its magnificent south colonnade, the facade of Trinity College, and the Royal Exchange were succeeded in 1791 by Gandon's Custom House, one of the noblest buildings in Europe. The Wide Streets Commissioners had laid out fine thoroughfares leading to Carlisle (now O'Connell) Bridge and the Phoenix Park offered citizens, rich and poor, ample facilities for recreation.

Poor there were in plenty. Behind the splendid wide streets and gracious buildings lay a warren of narrow, dirty and ill-lit lanes, inhabited in conditions of horrifying insanitariness by the labouring poor, and by small tradesmen and beggars.

Irish society was sharply divided on religious grounds. After the defeat of James II by England's

Protestant champion, William of Orange, at the battle
[4] of the Boyne in 1690, followed by 'Aughrim's great disaster' in 1691, the victors proceeded to make sure that the vanquished would not rise again. Land confiscations reduced the Catholic share of the land, brought down to 22 per cent by previous plantations, to 15 per cent. By Tone's time, it had fallen to 7 per cent. A body of legislation severely discriminating against Catholics was passed in the decades following the defeat of James. Under these Penal Laws, as they came to be known, Catholics could not join the army or navy, vote or be elected to parliament or hold any office of State. Catholics were forbidden to have schools of their own. The great majority had no education open to them save that of the hedge school. A Catholic could not buy land, obtain a mortgage on it, rent it out at a reasonable sum or inherit it save by division among the sons of the family. The Protestant historian, Lecky, wrote that 'the most worthless Protestant, if he had nothing else to boast of, at least found it pleasing that he was a member of a dominant race'.[1]

As a young Protestant barrister, Theobald Wolfe Tone came to play no small part in efforts to ameliorate the condition of the Catholics.

The college he entered in 1781, founded by Queen Elizabeth I under the style and title of 'The College of the Holy and Undivided Trinity, near Dublin' was incorporated on 3 March 1591, as 'the mother of an University'.[2] Socially, intellectually and politically, as the sole institution of higher education in the country, it was a nursery for the leaders in the professions, in government and in politics. The exclusion of Catholics, in force until 1793, meant that it catered only for an elite; the excluded majority, however talented or industrious, could aspire to no higher rank than that of merchant, farmer or prosperous tradesman. Most of the Irish aristocracy sent their sons to Trinity; a small minority preferred Oxford or Cambridge.

Tone's contemporaries and friends at Trinity included Charles Kendal Bushe, later Lord Chief Justice, the future Archbishop Magee and William Plunket, a future Lord Chancellor of Ireland.

Tone's career at Trinity was disappointing, although he won a scholarship in 1784. Military glory tempted him again before he was a year in Trinity and he urged his father to equip him as a volunteer so that he could join the British army to fight against the rebel colonists in America. His father refused and in a rage he abandoned his studies for a year and read only military books. As a result, he did not graduate until February 1786.

Towards the end of his second year, he narrowly escaped expulsion for taking part in a duel as second to an undergraduate named Anderson, who was shot in the head and killed by his opponent. Duelling was so fashionable at the time that it was said that no gentleman had taken his proper station in life until he had 'smelt powder'. No doubt, in these circumstances the authorities balked at expelling Tone, although he says himself that this adventure nearly drove him out of college a second time and forever.

Tone made his mark in University life outside the Examination Hall. In the Historical Society, founded by Edmund Burke, he won two medals for oratory, a further medal for an historical essay and was elected Auditor in his final year.

Contemporary descriptions of his appearance as a young man were unflattering. Jonah Barrington said 'his person was unfavourable; his countenance thin and sallow'.[3] A sister-in-law of Bushe's described him as 'a very slender, angular, rapid-moving man . . . eyes small, lively, bright; forehead very low, a thin face, sallow and pockmarked . . . laughed and talked fast

with enthusiasm about music and other innocent
[6] things.'[4] Despite the drawback of his appearance, his
infectious gaiety (a quality which he retained through
many dark hours) and animated conversation, which
sprung from his sparkling intelligence and vitality,
made an irresistible combination; men as well as
women were captivated by him. He had the indefin-
able attribute of charm and gained and kept the warm
affection of some of the finest men of his age.

The theatre flourished in Dublin in those years and
it was inevitable that a young man of Tone's lively
nature should be attracted to amateur drama. This led
him into an infatuation with the wife of Richard
Martin (later called 'Humanity Martin' by his friend,
George IV), Member of Parliament, owner of 200,000
acres in Connemara and so interested in drama that
he had installed a private theatre for amateur perfor-
mances in his house in Kildare Street. Tone and he
became very friendly and Tone, while still an undergraduate, went to live with the family, the house
being only a few minutes walk from Trinity. He also
spent some months in their Galway house. Mrs Martin
was beautiful, talented, wayward and an ardent
amateur actress. Propinquity, and Tone's susceptibility
to attractive women, had the natural result. He fell
violently in love with her and 'she made me miserable
for two years. She supposed she might amuse herself
innocently in observing the progress of this terrible
passion in an interesting young man of twenty.'[5] Tone
says that at length she fell in love with him too, but
that the affair never overstepped the bounds of virtue,
such was the purity of the extravagant affection he
bore her.

The affair was ended when Tone had a sharp disagreement with Martin on a matter having no connection whatever with Mrs Martin; the friendship ended
abruptly and he never saw her again.

Five and a half years later, in June 1790, Mrs Martin was seduced in Paris by a John Petrie, from [7] Essex. Her husband had been obliged, two months before, to break off from a continental tour with his family in order to attend to pressing estate business in London and then to fight an election in Ireland. A year later, he was awarded £10,000 damages in an action against Petrie for criminal conversation.[6] He subsequently divorced his wife.

Recalling all this as he sat writing his Journal in Paris in August 1796, Tone observed, 'It opened my eyes to many little circumstances that passed between her and me, and perhaps (as I now think), had my passion for her been less pure, it might have been not less agreeable ... my ignorance of the world prevented my availing myself of opportunities which a man more trained than I would not have let slip.' But he did not regret that he failed to betray the hospitality of his friend, 'Humanity Dick'. Philosophically, he consoled himself that though he suffered severely from the passion, he also benefited from it. 'The desire to render myself agreeable to a woman of elegant manners and a mind highly cultivated induced me to attend to a thousand little things and to endeavour to polish myself in a certain degree ... I considered myself on the whole considerably improved.' He adds disarmingly, 'As no human passion is proof against time and absence, in a few months I recovered my tranquillity.'[7]

He had the great gift of a resilient temperament; no man needed it more in later years. Within six months of being heartbroken at losing Mrs Martin, he had met, fallen in love with, run off with and married a girl of fifteen. He was just twenty-two and still an undergraduate with very uncertain prospects.

The girl, Matilda Witherington, lived in Grafton Street with her maternal grandfather, a rich old clergyman named Richard Fanning. On his daily stroll [8] after Commons with his friends from the college, Tone saw her sitting at her window and his affections were soon engaged. He contrived an introduction to the family and soon found that his feelings were returned, although as he engagingly records, 'certainly my appearance, neither then nor now, was much in my favour'. A runaway marriage followed in July 1785. After a honeymoon of a few days in May-nooth, the young couple returned to Dublin and were forgiven all round.

Marriage meant that he was no longer eligible for a fellowship, and it was decided that he should adopt the Bar as a career. To become a barrister in Dublin it was then necessary to spend two years in London keeping law terms. Nowhere in his autobiography does he say how his father, never prosperous and often hard-pressed, managed to give him an education much more expensive than that received by his brothers. It is not improbable that help came from Theobald Wolfe, the young squire of Blackhall after whom he was named. An obituary notice in *Faulkner's Journal* in 1798 states that Richard Griffith, a wealthy Member of Parliament, helped to finance his reading for the Bar. Any expectations that his wife's family would help was ended when Tone quarrelled with his brother-in-law whom he heartily disliked. There was an open breach with the Witheringtons and Tone and his wife went to live with his father at Bodenstown, Co. Kildare. His first child, a girl named Maria, was born there in 1786.

From Bodenstown, Tone set out for London and entered the Middle Temple in January 1787. It would be difficult to give an account of his two years there without using adjectives like 'irresponsible', 'improvi-dent', 'giddy' and 'selfish'. He sets it all down very frankly himself. 'After the first month I never opened a book, nor was I ever three times in Westminster Hall in my life . . . At the age of four and twenty, with a tolerable figure and address, in an idle and luxurious capital, it will not be supposed I was without adventures with the fair sex . . . I formed several delightful connections and as I was extremely discreet, I have the satisfaction to think that not one of those to whom I had the good fortune to render myself agreeable, ever suffered the slightest blemish in her reputation on my account.' He had three particular friends, all wealthy; two of whom, John Hall and Benjamin Phipps, had been his contemporaries at Trinity. The third, George Knox, helped to save Tone's life seven years later. Tone had chambers in the Temple, and despite his uncertain circumstances, 'contrived always to preserve the appearance of a gentleman.' His friends kept well-appointed establishments, with good wine and good books, and no doubt they heard the chimes at midnight many times together.

Early in 1788, Tone was joined in his chambers by his brother, William, only a year his junior, who had spent the previous six years in garrison duty on the island of St Helena. His enlistment term with the East India Company was now expired. He was the best of companions, and soon he and Phipps were inseparable. The friends made many agreeable expeditions, sometimes to a review, sometimes to see a ship of war launched, or to visit the Indiamen at Deptford. As far as the brothers were concerned, Tone observed, 'We were often without a guinea, but that never affected our spirits for a moment.'

He makes no reference to the theatre, although he certainly visited Drury Lane and saw the great Sarah Siddons, then at the height of her powers. In his Paris Journal of April 1796, he says that she far excelled the French actresses. He found French ballet and French comedians superior to English. Neither does

he mention English politics, although later in his autobiography he records that he had seen the English
parliament. However, his account of those years in
London was written eight years later, after he had
gone through many vicissitudes, and characteristically
he dwells principally on the companionship and happiness he enjoyed at the time as a relatively carefree
young man in a foreign city.

He exerted himself sufficiently to write several
articles and reviews for the *European Magazine,* which
earned him fifty pounds, and collaborated with two
friends in a burlesque novel, *Belmont Castle,* which
did not find a publisher until 1790, when Byrne of
Grafton Street, Dublin, printed it.

As he disliked the law intensely, it was natural that
his fertile mind should turn to some other scheme for
winning fame and fortune. With his brother and
Phipps, he prepared a plan for establishing a military
colony on the Sandwich (now the Hawaiian) Islands,
discovered by Captain Cook some ten years previously.
They spent the early summer of 1788 perfecting their
plan and then in August, Tone prepared a memorial
for submission to the Prime Minister, Pitt, showing
how the colony could harass Spanish traders and have
other advantages for England. He delivered it in person at Downing Street, but Pitt, if indeed he ever read
it, treated it with complete indifference, to Tone's
fury.

Another blow followed. He received a letter from
his father to the effect that he was on the verge of
bankruptcy. Tone's own affairs, he said, were extremely embarassed at the time. In a state of desperation and rage, he determined to enlist as a soldier in
the India Company and quit Europe for ever. His
brother pleaded with him, but seeing that his mind
was made up, William said that he, too, would enlist.
On presenting themselves at the India Office, they

were told that the season was passed and that no more ships would be sent out until the following March. [11] Tone's account of the episode ends, 'Had it been the month of March instead of September we should most infallibly have gone off; and, in that case, I should most probably at this hour be carrying a brown musket on the coast of Coromandel'. As to his wife and child, he was leaving them to the mercy of her family, who, might, he hoped, be kinder to her when he was removed.

Towards the end of 1788, he had kept the required terms at the Temple by dining three days in each term in the common hall, and he addressed himself to the necessity of earning a living. Through a friend, he opened communication with his wife's grandfather, Mr Fanning, who obligingly agreed to supply £500 to enable him to begin practice at the Irish Bar. So, with his brother, he left London and they arrived at his father's house at Bodenstown on Christmas Day, 1788. He found the family in good health, except for his wife, who, he says, had grown delicate, principally from the anxiety about the uncertainty of her position. A few days later he went to Dublin with his wife and child and was reconciled with the Witheringtons. Mr Fanning was as good as his word and paid the £500 at once. Tone took lodgings in Clarendon Street, spent £100 on law books, and determined to apply himself to his profession, although he said that when he was leaving London he knew exactly as much about law as he did of necromancy. He took the degree of Bachelor of Laws in February 1789, was called to the Bar in the following Trinity term and went on the Leinster Circuit.

2

Dublin, the Irish Bar and the United Irishmen

On his first circuit, Tone succeeded in nearly clearing his expenses. His dislike of the law continued, however, and he was unable to apply himself to it with any diligence. That year, his father lost a Chancery suit against his brother, Jonathan. He was obliged to sell his remaining property, and was saved from complete destitution only by the fortunate chance of obtaining a post as Inspector of Globes under the Dublin Paving Board at £50 a year. Tone's own dwindling funds were further depleted in unsuccessful efforts to avert the ruin of his father.

Several of Tone's friends had advanced their prospects by pamphleteering, a popular method at the time. He decided to try his hand and in a few days composed his first pamphlet, *A Review of the Conduct of Administration during the Seventh Session of Parliament,* signing himself 'An Independent Irish Whig'. A slashing attack on the government, it naturally pleased the Whig opposition. The Northern Whig Club reprinted it in April 1790, and circulated it as election propaganda. When they discovered that Tone was the author, they elected him a member of their club and he was introduced to George Ponsonby, nominal leader of the opposition (the real leader was Henry Grattan). Furthermore, he received a strong hint that the Whigs would not always be out of power and that he would not be forgotten when they had seats in parliament to bestow on their supporters. As a practical earnest of benefits to come, he was retained as Whig counsel in an election petition at a fee of eighty guineas, a very [13] welcome addition to his funds as his wife's fortune was then nearly exhausted.

This modest success seemed to indicate the opening of a political career, but Ponsonby showed no great desire to advance Tone in Whig circles. But for the first time, it seems, Tone's interest had been awakened in the history of his country. To his friend, Sir Lawrence Parsons, afterwards Lord Rosse, an independent Member of Parliament, he gave the credit for opening his mind to Ireland's lack of real independence, and for laying the blame for that situation on the connection with England.

The so-called legislative independence won by Grattan and the Volunteers for the Irish parliament in 1782 was illusory. Of the 300 seats in the Irish House of Commons, 172 were the property of fewer than one hundred individuals. One-third of the entire House were pensioners or place-men of the Crown. Crown patronage ensured an almost automatic majority in the House. The government was not answerable to the Irish parliament, as its members were appointed by, and accountable to, the English ministry of the day. It was entirely a Protestant parliament; Catholics could neither sit in it, nor vote for it. In a word, it was corrupt, non-representative and sectarian, a creature of its English masters.

Tone's second pamphlet reflected the development of his political thinking. England and Spain seemed on the verge of war. Grattan and his supporters in parliament, while agitating for independence in domestic affairs, had always accepted that Ireland should support England's foreign policy. Tone challenged this view, claiming that Ireland's interest should be the sole criterion in determining her attitude, and questioning why Ireland should go to war with Spain with whom she had no quarrel. He did not call into [14] question the position of the King as King of Ireland. His pamphlet, signed 'Hibernicus' and entitled *An Enquiry how far Ireland is bound, of right, to embark in the impending contest on the side of Great Britain,* aroused the rage of the establishment, and the printer, Byrne, hastily suppressed it. The general election of May 1790 brought no change in government. When parliament met in July, it unanimously pledged support to the King, and voted £200,000 to put Ireland in a state of defence. However, war was averted later in the year by Pitt's diplomacy.

About this time, in the Strangers' Gallery in the House of Commons, Tone made the acquaintance of Thomas Russell, a young officer of twenty-three, home on half-pay from India, and they quickly became, and remained, fast friends. Tone's uncertain prospects were further dimmed by a quarrel with his wife's family, fomented, according to him, by his wife's brother, with the aim of ensuring that Mrs Tone received no further share of her grandfather's fortune. Old Mr Fanning died shortly afterwards, without mentioning her in his will. Matilda had had a second child and was expecting a third. Her health continued delicate and her physician ordered salt water bathing. Tone rented 'a little box of a house, at Irishtown', where they spent the long vacation of 1790. In his Journal, Tone gives a delightful account of their idyllic summer. 'I recall with transport the happy days we spent together during that period; the delicious dinners in the preparation of which my wife, Russell and myself were all engaged; the afternoon walks; the discussions we had as we lay stretched on the grass. It was delightful!'

A war with Spain still seemed imminent and Tone bethought himself of his scheme to colonise the Sandwich Islands. He mentioned it to Russell and as they had nothing better to do, they prepared a new draft which they dispatched to the Duke of Richmond, [15] Master of the Ordnance. He gave them a civil reply, praising 'the perspicuous and compendious manner' in which they stated their proposal, but referring them to Grenville, Secretary of State for the Home Office, under which the War Office then came. The Home Office duly replied, in effect stating that they had more important business on hand.

Meanwhile, Russell had been promoted ensign on full pay in the 64th regiment of foot. After a fare-well dinner at Irishtown, which he helped to prepare dressed in a very fine suit of laced regimentals, he left to take up duty in Belfast where his regiment was then stationed. There he became friendly with an American, Thomas Digges, an adventurer whose acquaintance with Tone and himself had disastrous consequences for both young men.

The Tones returned to town for the winter of 1790, Mrs Tone's health greatly improved. His mind remain-ing engrossed with politics, Tone tried to found a political club, but it lasted only three or four months. The members included William Drennan, poet, medical doctor and a founder of the United Irishmen; Peter Burrowes, a barrister; Whitley Stokes, fellow of Trinity College; and Thomas Addis Emmet, a barrister and elder brother of Robert Emmet, leader of the rising of 1803. The club failed because it had no clear objec-tive and personal incompatibilities soon showed them-selves. Nevertheless, it brought Tone into close contact with those four men who had a strong influence on his burgeoning political thought.

The event that above all influenced men's thoughts at that time was the French Revolution. Public interest, already strongly aroused, was brought to a pitch by the publication in 1790 of Edmund Burke's *Reflec-tions on the Revolution in France,* and of Thomas

Paine's response, *Rights of Man*, in February 1791.
[16] Tone wrote later in his Journal that 'this controversy, and the gigantic event which gave rise to it, changed in an instant the politics of Ireland. The nation was fairly divided into two great parties, the Aristocrats and the Democrats. . . . I was a Democrat from the very commencement.' The monarchy and the institutions which surrounded it no longer seemed unassailable. The ideas of republicanism and separatism appeared to be realities capable of achievement. This was heady wine for a subject people.

In Belfast, Russell was soon on friendly terms with members of the Volunteers and was elected to one of their political clubs. He sold his commission on 30 June 1791, and left the army. It seems that he did this in order to save Digges from his creditors by lending him £200. In October 1791, when Tone first visited Belfast, Digges was constantly in their company. They discussed their political ideas freely with him and both conceived an uncritical admiration of him. However, Digges never repaid Russell. The loss of £200, a substantial sum in those days, must have been a crippling blow, especially to a man of no fortune like Russell. The following year, Digges was caught stealing a wig in a shop in Glasgow while on a visit with friends from Belfast. He escaped the law but was never seen in Belfast again.

The idea that Protestant Dissenters should unite with the Catholics in pressing for reform had always appealed to the more radical thinkers among the Volunteers. The fall of the Bastille was to be celebrated in Belfast on 14 July 1791 by a Volunteer meeting. At Russell's request, Tone drafted suitable resolutions for the occasion, including one favouring the inclusion of Catholics in any reforms. In a covering letter to Russell, Tone wrote, 'I have not said one word that looks like a wish for separation, though I give it to you and your friends as my most decided opinion that such an event would be a regeneration of their country.'[8] When this letter came into the posession of the authorities some years later, they made deadly use of it against Tone, the United Irishmen and the Catholic Committee. Both Drennan and Russell later alleged that it was Digges who gave it to the government.

Tone's resolution in favour of the Catholic cause was dropped. He noted bitterly that 'the Northerners sought rather a monopoly than an extension of liberty ... contrary to all justice and expediency.' At this point in his Journal, written five years later, he sets down the words by which he is most remembered. 'I soon formed my theory. . . . To subvert the tyranny of our execrable government, to break the connection with England, the never-failing source of all our political evils, and to assert the independence of my country, these were my objects. To unite the whole people of Ireland, to abolish the memory of past dissensions, and to substitute the common name of Irishman, in place of the denominations of Protestant, Catholic and Dissenter, these were my means.'

He then reviewed the position of the three great sects, as he calls them, in Ireland, Protestants, Catholics and Dissenters, in relation to the achievement of his aims. The Protestants, he noted, would never adhere to any policy that would imperil their entrenched power and privileges. The support of the Catholics could be taken for granted, since they had nothing to lose and everything to gain from change. So he proposed to address himself to the Dissenters as fertile soil for his ideas, although the rejection of his resolution showed him that many of them still harboured a strong prejudice against Catholics. The result was his best pamphlet, entitled *An Argument on behalf of the Catholics of Ireland*, published in September 1791 under the pseudonym, 'A Northern Whig', as he was a [18] member of the Northern Whig Club. Its authorship was soon acknowledged. Having rehearsed the ills which flowed from the existing system of government and pointed out the absolute necessity of parliamentary reform, he developed his main argument, that any reform that did not grant the elective franchise to the Roman Catholics would be neither practicable nor just. He castigated the so-called 'revolution' of 1782, which purported to give legislative independence to the Irish parliament as 'the most bungling, imperfect business that ever threw ridicule on a lofty epithet by assuming it unworthily'.

His explicit profession of loyalty to the King as King of Ireland has been taken as evidence that his republicanism and his separatism came late in his career. But also in this pamphlet he rails furiously against those who contended that Ireland could not exist as an independent state. The idea that the King of England could have certain external functions in relation to an independent Ireland was not repugnant to some republicans close to our own times. And Tone had given expression to the separatist idea in the letter which he had written to Russell the previous July.

He argued little, he said, on the abstract right of the people to reform their legislature, 'for, after Paine, who will or who need, to be heard on that subject?'

At the time he wrote this pamphlet, he tells, he was not acquainted with a single Catholic.

The pamphlet was an immediate success and gained him the notice of the Catholic Committee, a respectable and conservative organisation founded about 1760. Its leading members, bishops, Catholic peers and country gentlemen, had hitherto shown little stomach for confrontation with authority and walked in fear of antagonising the establishment. But in John

Keogh, a middle-class merchant, the radical element in the committee found a leader who welcomed Tone's vigorous espousal of their cause. [19]

The pamphlet was also hailed by the Dissenters of the North, who invited Tone to visit Belfast in October 1791, to assist in founding a new political organisation. The idea of the organisation had been mooted earlier that year by William Drennan. No progress had been made until Tone's pamphlet had fired the imagination of the Belfast Volunteers, who already, he tells us, had made Paine's *Rights of Man* their Koran and who were watching the progress of the French Revolution with excited approval. A secret committee had been formed to organise the new society and both Tone and Russell were made members. The name decided on was the Society of United Irishmen. Resolutions and a manifesto drafted by Tone were adopted at the inaugural meeting on 18 October 1791. The resolutions called for a cordial union among all the people of Ireland to counteract the weight of English influence in the government of the country, and for complete and radical parliamentary reform. It was affirmed that no reform would be practicable, efficacious or just which did not include Irishmen of every religious persuasion.

Meetings of the society were private but it did not become a secret society until three years later, when its character changed completely. At the beginning, it was an open reform club with radical principles.

Tone and Russell remained in Belfast for more than a fortnight, until 25 October, and enjoyed themselves immensely, spending days and nights in animated discussion, drinking a great deal of wine and forming fast friendships with the leading spirits in the new society. These included Samuel Neilson, who, by his active leadership in the secret committee which had organised the United Irishmen could be said to be the founder of the society, or at least to have brought to active life the ideas thrown up by Drennan. They were entertained most hospitably, and though Tone records heated, and sometimes bitter, after-dinner arguments on the Catholic question, it does not seem to have come home to him how deep was the divide between Dissenters and Catholics. At one dinner, a dissenting clergyman of standing, the Rev. William Bruce, repeated three objections to reform for the Catholics, which clearly constituted his creed on the subject. These objections were, 'first, danger to true religion, inasmuch as the Roman Catholics would, if emancipated, establish an inquisition; second, danger to property by reviving the Court of Claims, and admitting any evidence to substantiate Catholic titles; third, danger, generally, of throwing the power into their hands, which would make this a Catholic government, incapable of enjoying or extending liberty.' All of the Dissenters at the table agreed with Bruce, while at the same time protesting their liberality and good wishes to the Roman Catholics. These views, of course, made the resolutions of the United Irishmen appear as empty rhetoric and their chief tactic of uniting Catholic and Dissenter as an idle dream, but Tone's optimistic temperament was not dashed.

In his diary he records, on his second day in Belfast, christening Russell, 'P.P., Clerk of this Parish.' Belfast he called 'Blefescu', and, in turn, Russell called him 'my friend Mr John Hutton'. They had late nights and remorseful mornings. 'P.P. very drunk. . . . P.P. in the blue devils — thinks he is losing his faculties, glad he has any to lose . . . all arguments over a bottle foolish . . . Very ill-natured to P.P. P.P. patient.'

It was agreed that, on his return to Dublin, Tone should get in touch with Napper Tandy, a prominent radical, who as a Volunteer had commanded the approaches to the Houses of Parliament when their independence was announced in May 1782. A Dublin club of the United Irishmen was founded on 9 November 1791, with Simon Butler, a barrister and brother of Lord Mountgarret, as chairman and Napper Tandy as secretary. No oath was required but every member was called on to take the following 'Test': 'I, A. B., in the presence of God, do pledge myself to my country that I will use all my abilities and influence in the attainment of an adequate and impartial representation of the Irish nation in Parliament, and as a means of absolute and immediate necessity in the attainment of this chief good of Ireland, I will endeavour as much as lies in my ability, to forward a brotherhood of affection, an identity of interests, a communion of rights and a union of power among Irishmen of all religious persuasions, without which every reform must be partial, not national, inadequate to the wants, delusive to the wishes and insufficient for the freedom and happiness of this country.'

The society held its meetings in the Tailors' Hall, Back Lane, which runs from Nicholas Street to Cornmarket. In *Ireland Sixty Years Ago,* John Edward Walsh describes how an undergraduate once walked unchallenged into the Hall and there saw Tone, Tandy and Hamilton Rowan. Tone was 'a slight, effeminate-looking man, with a hatchet face, a long aquiline nose, rather handsome and genteel-looking, with lank straight hair combed down on his sickly red cheek, exhibiting a face the most insignificant and mindless that could be imagined. His mode of speaking was in correspondence with his face and person. It was polite and gentlemanly, but totally devoid of anything like energy or vigour. I set him down as a worthy, good-natured, flimsy man, in whom there was no harm, and as the least likely person in the world to do mischief to the state.'

Tandy was the very opposite looking character. He

was 'the ugliest man I ever gazed on. He had a dark, [22] yellow, truculent-looking countenance, a long drooping nose, rather sharpened at the point. . . . a remarkable hanging-down look.' Not so Hamilton Rowan. 'I thought him not only the most handsome, but the largest man I had ever seen.' Tone and Tandy looked like pygmies beside him. 'His ample and capacious forehead seemed the seat of thought and energy; while with such an external to make him feared, he had a courtesy that excited love and confidence.'[9]

The impressions of a freshman at Trinity College, with scarcely any experience of the world, must be taken with caution. Tone was then twenty-eight and was very conscious of his failings as a public speaker. His diary for 8 October 1792 laments his poor showing at a public meeting, 'not only modest, but sheepish . . . made a poor exhibition . . . must try and mend.'

Other prominent members of the Dublin society were the brothers Henry and John Sheares from Cork; Whitley Stokes and Thomas Addis Emmet, who had been members of the earlier short-lived political society founded by Tone in 1790; Oliver Bond, woollen merchant; William McNevin and John Lawless, medical doctors; and Arthur O'Connor, of a wealthy merchant family. Like the Belfast members, they came from the comfortable middle classes, an exception being Lord Edward FitzGerald, and in the North, Jemmy Hope, a linen weaver. Most were Protestants, although large numbers of Catholics soon joined.

Tone wrote 'The Club was scarcely formed before I lost all pretensions to anything like influence in their measures, a circumstance which at first mortified me not a little'. Whether this was due to his being overshadowed by the more forceful personality of Tandy, who virtually took charge from an early date, or to his precarious financial circumstances, which must have weighed on his mind, one cannot say, nor does he advance any reason himself. However, his active mind was soon occupied with another though closely related cause, the struggle of the Catholics for their rights.

He came forward early in 1792 to champion the United Irishmen when the Solicitor-General, the notorious John Toler, later 1st Earl of Norbury, made contemptuous reference to them in the Commons. After some exchanges between Toler and Tandy, the House ordered the arrest of Tandy for breach of privilege and he went into hiding. Tone became alarmed that the society would be disgraced if the members did not stand their ground. It was arranged that Hamilton Rowan should become acting chairman in place of Butler and that Tone should take the office of secretary. Resolutions were passed stressing the constitutional character of the objects of the society and denouncing Toler's action as an abuse of parliamentary privilege. The resolutions, signed by Rowan and Tone, were published in the newspapers and thousands of copies were printed and distributed. The House ignored this action, but on the last day of the session, Tandy was arrested, brought to the Bar of the House and ordered by the Speaker to be jailed in Newgate. Rowan and Tone appeared in the gallery, attired in gaudy Whig club uniforms to ensure that they would be noticed, and perhaps hoping that a challenge or a prosecution would give them an opportunity to show their mettle. But no notice was taken of them. Tandy was released the same day after parliament was prorogued. The next day, the House was accidentally burnt to the ground and the members had little thought to give to Tone and his associates. Tone, for his part, was well satisfied that their actions had brought credit and public support to the society.

Shortly afterwards, he was again approached by the Whigs. Their spokesman, a barrister, reproached

Tone for supporting the policies of the United Irishmen, indicating that the Whigs regarded him as one of
their own. Tone indignantly rejected any suggestion
that the Whigs had any claim on him and said that if
Ponsonby desired his support, he should show so
openly. Further, he had no intention of abandoning
the principles he had so publicly supported and that
Ponsonby could be so informed. Tone put the blame
for the enmity shown to him by Ponsonby three years
later, during the Jackson affair, on Ponsonby's rage
at his overtures having been so summarily repulsed
by a penniless barrister.

Penniless, indeed, and in his own words, his affairs
were nearly desperate. But his pamphlets and his association with the United Irishmen had made him well
known, particularly for his championship of the
Catholics. It was not without cause, then, that he was
approached by the Catholic Committee in the spring
or early summer of 1792.

3
The Catholic Committee

Concessions to the Roman Catholics began in 1750 when they were admitted to the lesser grades of the army. In 1771 the Bogland Act enabled them to take leases for sixty-one years of not more than fifty acres of unprofitable land, to be free of taxes for seven years. The first Catholic Relief Act of 1778 enabled them to buy property again and in 1782 a further Relief Act admitted Catholics fully to the same rights of property and leasehold in land as Protestants. But Catholics were still precluded from voting, sitting in parliament or holding any office of state.

The Catholic Committee was dominated by Lords Trimleston, Kenmare, Fingall and Gormanston. They did not like being associated with men of trade, that is, the properous merchants, who, with the bishops, made up the rest of the committee. The leader of the radicals on the committee was John Keogh, and this shrewd municipal politician rallied the merchants to his side. They resented bitterly their exclusion from the professions and from offices of state. In January 1792 this radical element succeeded in forcing the lords to resign from the committee and at once embarked on an active campaign to secure full civil rights for Catholics. A petition for such rights was presented to parliament but was summarily rejected. The committee was called 'a rabble of obscure porter-drinking mechanics, without property, pretensions or influence, who met in holes and

corners'. A petition from six hundred citizens of Belfast asking that Roman Catholics be put on an equal
footing with their Protestant fellow-subjects met with
the same fate. Sir Boyle Roche described these
Northerners as 'a disorderly set of people whom no
king can govern and no God can please.'

Richard Burke, son of the famous Edmund, had
been employed by the committee as their agent in
this business. Dissatisfied with his performance, they
terminated his appointment, softening the blow by
paying him £2,000 for his services. Tone was then
appointed agent, with the title of assistant secretary
and a stipend of £200 for the period until the rising
of parliament. This was far from munificent, but there
was a hope of further remuneration and this hope was
fulfilled in due course.

John Keogh was born in 1740 in poor circumstances and began life as a small tradesman in Dublin.
His business prospered and he gained wide influence
among his fellow-Catholics. Tone did not care for him,
and makes this very clear in his Journal. He christened
him 'Gog'. Richard McCormick and Edward Byrne,
prominent men in the committee, were dubbed
'Magog' and 'The Vintner' respectively. Napper
Tandy became 'The Tribune'.

The committee resolved to show their denigrators
in parliament that they did, in fact, truly represent
the Catholics of Ireland. Plans were prepared to hold
a convention in Dublin towards the end of 1792 to be
attended by Catholics from all over the country who
would be elected by parish delegates. The announcement of this plan created a storm of protest; it was
denounced in furious resolutions by the grand juries
all over the country. The government, alarmed at the
prospect of an agitation supported by three million
Irish subjects, took steps to alienate the bishops by
representing that the holding of the convention would

be an usurpation of parliamentary privilege bordering on treason. But the committee obtained written opinions from Simon Butler and Beresford Burton, two leading King's Counsel, that their proceedings were perfectly legal. Copies were widely distributed and printed in the newspapers. The committee held their ground. 'At first', wrote Tone, 'we were like young soldiers, a little stunned with the noise, but after a few rounds we began to look about us, and seeing nobody drop with all this furious cannonade, we took courage and determined to return the fire.' On behalf of the committee he defended the Catholic position in a series of vigorous replies to these attacks.

The Belfast Volunteers proposed to celebrate the third anniversary of the fall of the Bastille on 14 July 1792. Tone had been made a member of the first company and he set out for Belfast on 9 July with Whitley Stokes, member of the Dublin United Irishmen and fellow of Trinity College. In his diary Tone calls him 'The Keeper of the College Lions'. The Volunteers paraded on Bastille Day, with Tone resplendent in uniform. The parade was followed by a meeting in the Linen Hall, at which two addresses were passed, one, drafted by Dr Drennan, to the people of France, the other, drafted by Tone, to the people of Ireland. Tone's address included the assertion that 'no reform would answer to this gathering's ideas of utility or justice, which should not equally include all sects and denominations of Irishmen.' Keogh, McCormick and others from the Catholic Committee attended to show their solidarity with their friends in the North. At the banquet that evening Tone broke his glass thumping the table and went to bed 'God knows how or when', delirious with happiness. Two days later, the Catholics were entertained to dinner by the United Irishmen and Tone noted, 'chequered at the head of the table, a Dissenter and a Catholic.

Delightful!'

Belfast hospitality was as warm as ever, and the new liberal attitude of the Presbyterians towards the Catholics was heartening, but Tone missed the companionship of Russell, who had been rescued from penury by an appointment early in 1792 as magistrate in Dungannon. This had come about most probably through the good offices of George Knox, friend of Tone from his London days. Tone laments in his diary, 'All this day dull as a post; no P.P. Sad! Sad!'

Outbreaks of agrarian violence had become a feature of rural life in the second half of the eighteenth century, springing from the desperate struggle for land which accompanied population increase. Catholics were generally prepared to offer higher rents and accept a lower standard of living than Protestants, and the violence became sectarian. Protestant 'Peep o' Day Boys' and Catholic 'Defenders' engaged in sporadic warfare. At Rathfriland in Co. Down several bloody encounters had taken place, with loss of life. Tone set off with Samuel Neilson and a companion to see what could be done to bring peace. They were joined by representatives of the Catholics and some local gentlemen. Tone claimed to find that the Protestants were the aggressors and that the Catholics did nothing worse than meet in large numbers and fire powder, foolish certainly but not wicked. It was agreed that they should desist from parades and firing.

Tone returned to Dublin on 20 July 1792. He had become friendly with Grattan and was invited several times that summer to Grattan's house at Tinnehinch, an easy day's ride from Dublin. Grattan's liberal attitude towards the Catholics had always been in advance of that of the majority of his fellow Whigs: he had advocated that they should get the vote and be admitted to all offices of state. At one of these meetings in Tinnehinch, he drew Tone aside and told him that it was the wish of himself and his colleagues that all communication between them should be through Tone. This seemed to Tone to be a wise precaution against the committee being exposed to the charge of being tools of the Whig opposition, and he was especially pleased that Grattan should show such confidence in him, as the Whigs had refused to have any communication with his predecessor, Richard Burke. But John Keogh took this amiss. His vanity was wounded and to mollify him, Tone discreetly suggested that the arrangement should be kept secret. In this, Tone was following a line of conduct he had laid down for himself since his appointment as assistant secretary. He had resolved to be a faithful servant of the committee, never to press his own views or to object to criticism of his memoranda or reject suggested amendments. In a word, he was devoted to the Catholic cause and determined to win the trust and respect of the committee. In this, he was highly successful.

In May 1792, Tone was in correspondence with Colonel H. Barry, a close friend of Lord and Lady Moira, Whig aristrocrats whose house in Dublin was the chief meeting place of the Whigs. Barry was trying to secure a lieutenancy for Russell, who was unhappy with his position in Dungannon, and also a post for Tone as secretary to General Lord Rawdon, eldest son of Lord Moira, who was contemplating a political career. Both requests failed. Rawdon supported the Catholic Committee and was of good service to them when they went to London with their petition later that year. Tone's employment with the committee did not begin formally until 24 July and was temporary. There is nothing inconsistent in his endeavour to secure a post with a Whig as liberal as Lord Rawdon.

The committee was requested to send someone to [30] Ballinasloe, Co. Galway, to meet the Catholic gentry of Mayo and Galway, in order to counteract the influence of Denis Browne, member of parliament for Mayo and brother of Lord Altamont. Browne opposed the holding of a Catholic Convention, although otherwise a supporter of Catholic claims. Tone left Dublin at eight in the evening on 5 October 1792 in a post-chaise, accompanied by a Dublin merchant named Tom Braughall. At the gate of the Phoenix Park they were stopped by some footpads but they had two cases of pistols in the chaise. Tone threatened to shoot the postillion if he did not drive on. The footpads took fright and ran off.

At Athlone they met Dr French, Catholic bishop of Elphin, 'a spirited fellow and much the gentleman'. But the parish priest at Ballinasloe he found 'a sad, vulgar booby'. The victuals were bad, the wine poisonous and the beds execrable. He dined with the Catholics on the Sunday evening and found them 'dull as ten thousand devils.' But things improved the next day when he attended a good meeting presided over by Lord French, 'a fine young fellow.' Having arranged to send an emissary, James Plunket, to meet the Mayo gentry, he dined with Plunket and eight Galway bucks. 'All civil, but intolerably dull. Handicapping, wagers, horse-racing, swapping.' He arrived back in Dublin on 11 October, well satisfied with the results of his mission. He was confident that Galway and Mayo, 'the two great Catholic counties in Ireland and the cream and flower of the Catholic gentry', would elect delegates to the convention. And so it proved.

He still maintained his contacts with the United Irishmen and describes a dinner on 1 November with a group of their leaders. 'Talk a great deal of tactics and treason. Mr Hutton (Tone) grows warm with the subject; very much surprised, on looking down the table, to see two glasses before him; finds, on looking at Hamilton Rowan, that he has got four eyes . . . [31] perfectly sober, but perceives that every one else is getting very drunk; essays to walk across the room, but finds it impossible to move rectilineally, proceeding entirely from his having taken a sprig of watercress with his bread at dinner.' Next morning, he is 'as sick as Demogorgon; purpose to leave off watercress with my bread'.

He was at the courts on 9 November and noted with satisfaction a change in the attitude of the Bar on the Catholic question, with almost everybody favourable. His brethern of the wig and gown had some good-natured fun at his expense, calling him 'Marat' and applying to him for protection in the approaching rebellion. 'Exceeding good laughing'.

The preparations for the convention went forward in November, Tone working hard on the drafting of resolutions and an address to the King. By the middle of the month, delegates had been elected in twenty-five counties and the principal cities, and the committee was confident that the remainder would come in before the meeting-day.

The convention, the first representative body of Catholics to meet in Ireland since the parliament of James II over a century before, assembled in Tailors' Hall, Back Lane, Dublin on 3 December 1792. This was the hall in which the first Dublin United Irishmen held their meetings. The delegates numbered 235, and included Dr Troy, archbishop of Dublin, and Dr Moylan, bishop of Cork. Two resolutions were passed unanimously. The first read, 'That the Catholic peers, prelates and delegates, chosen by the people, are the only power competent to speak the sense of the Catholics of Ireland.' The second went, 'That a petition be presented to his Majesty, stating our grievances and praying relief.' Still smarting from the summary

rejection by the Irish parliament of their petition of
the previous January, the committee determined to
by-pass the Dublin administration and to approach
the King through Henry Dundas, the English Secretary
of State for Home Affairs. Five delegates were
appointed to go to London. They were Keogh, Byrne,
Devereux, Bellew and Sir Thomas French, that is, two
merchants and three country gentlemen. Tone accompanied them as secretary. Before adjourning, the convention passed a vote of thanks to Tone for 'the faithful discharge of his duty as our agent, and for the zeal,
spirit and abilities which he has manifested in the
cause of the Catholics of Ireland.'

The delegates were instructed to insist on seeing
the King in person, to ask for the total removal of all
penal and restrictive laws affecting Irish Catholics and
'to take an hotel and make a superb appearance'.
They decided to travel via Belfast, as the shorter sea-
crossing would be surer. They received a great welcome in Belfast, the people unharnessing the horses
from their carriage and drawing it with loud cheers.
Lord Rawdon met them on their arrival in London
and entertained them repeatedly 'in a style of splendid
magnificence'. Dundas tried to prevent them from
seeing the King but they stood firm and through
Rawdon's influence, they were presented at St James's
Palace on 2 January 1793. They then delivered into
the King's own hands the petition of his Catholic subjects of Ireland. Tone describes the scene thus: 'Their
appearance was splendid, and they met with what is
called in the language of courts, a most gracious reception: that is, his Majesty was pleased to say a few
words to each of the delegates in his turn. In those
colloquies, the matter is generally of little interest,
the manner is all; and with the manner of the Sover-
eign, the delegates had every reason to be content.'

Satisfied with what they had accomplished, although

without any definite undertakings from Dundas, they returned to Dublin, leaving Devereux in London as a kind of Chargé d'Affaires.

The time was ripe to press strongly for full civil rights for the Catholics. On 3 December 1792, the day the convention had assembled in Dublin, the French National Convention moved to put Louis XVI on trial. It became clear to the British government that war with France was inevitable. An Ireland seething with discontent presented constant danger of invasion by France, with probable help from within the country. It seemed imperative to the British that Irish opinion should be conciliated. Edmund Burke, who detested Revolutionary France and all it stood for, was exerting all his powerful influence to grant concessions to the Catholics so as to win them over from sympathy with French aspirations for liberty. But John Fitzgibbon, later Lord Clare, the powerful Lord Chancellor of Ireland, was vehemently opposed to the granting of any concessions that might weaken the Protestant ascendancy at a time when the established order all over Europe was being threatened by revolutionary ideas. He maintained that Catholic emancipation would inevitably lead to parliamentary reform. A parliament elected on reformed lines would sooner or later break the connection with England, and so bring about anarchy in Ireland and danger to England. This argument contained an ironical echo of Tone's declaration of his own theory.

Matters seemed to be progressing favourably for the Catholic Committee when at the opening of the Irish parliament on 10 January 1793 the Lord Lieutenant's speech included the sentence 'His Majesty trusts that the situation of His Majesty's Catholic subjects will engage your serious attention and in the consideration of this subject relies on the wisdom and liberality of his Parliament.'

But the Irish administration was not prepared to [34] yield easily. In Robert Hobart, Chief Secretary, they had an experienced and able, not to say wily, negotiator. On 21 January 1793, the day Louis XVI was guillotined in Paris, the Catholic Committee sent Keogh, Byrne, McDonnell and Sir Thomas French to Hobart to tell him that nothing short of unlimited emancipation would satisfy the Catholics. Tone records 'They return in about an hour, extremely dissatisfied with each other, and after diverse mutual recriminations, it appears, by the confession of all parties, that, so far from discharging their commission, they had done directly the reverse; for the result of their conversation with the Secretary was, that he had declared explicitly against the whole measure, and they had given him reason, in consequence, to think that the Catholics would acquiesce contentedly in a half-one. Sad! Sad! I am surprised at Sir T. French, for, as for merchants, I begin to see they are no great hands at revolutions.' A series of acrimonious subcommittee meetings followed, at which Tone made valiant efforts to stiffen the resolve of Keogh and the rest. But the pass had been sold and the ground lost could not be recovered. A curious aspect of the affair was the bold and determined conduct of the delegates when confronting the English Minister and their ignominious collapse when they came to deal with Hobart in Dublin. Subservience to the Irish administration was ingrained and the habit of respectful acceptance of their edicts could not be shaken off overnight. Keogh himself had said not long before that you could recognise a Catholic in the towns by the way he slunk along the streets.

A bill to grant relief of Catholic disabilities eventually passed both Houses of Parliament and received the Royal Assent on 9 April 1793. It gave Catholics the right to vote on a forty-shilling freehold, that is, on the same terms as Protestants, and also the right to bear arms for self-defence, subject to a property qualification. Trinity College was opened to them, including the professorships, except that of divinity. They became fully eligible for the magistracy, for jury service, and for membership of bodies corporate. Civil and military posts and places of trust or profit were thrown open to them, subject to a long list of exceptions, which included high offices of state, the judicial bench, King's Counsel, sheriffs and army generals. They were still excluded from seats in parliament. This exclusion rankled with Tone and with the country gentry especially. Tone's indignation is very clear. 'By their exclusion from the two houses of Parliament', he wrote, 'the whole body of the Catholic gentry of Ireland, a high-spirited race of men, are insulted and disgraced, thrown down from the level of their fortune and their talents, and branded with a mark of subjugation, the last relic of interested bigotry. Will they not say that they have received just so much liberty as will enable them to serve the interests of others, to be useful freeholders and convenient voters, artificers of the greatness and power in which they must not share, subaltern instruments in the elevation of those who their honest pride tells them are in no respect better than themselves?'

War broke out between France and England in February 1793 while the bill was being debated in parliament. The British government under Pitt adopted their traditional policy in time of crisis of combining conciliation with repression. Volunteering was suppressed, a paid militia under direct government control was set up and a Convention Act was passed making illegal the holding of assemblies claiming to represent any large body of the people.

While the bill was being debated in the Commons, a Secret Committee of the House of Lords was set up at the instigation of Lord Chancellor Fitzgibbon, to enquire into the causes of the disturbances which had taken place in certain counties. Witnesses could be compelled to give evidence on oath. As became clear when their report was published, the aim of this committee was to discredit the Catholic Committee and the United Irishmen by implicating them in outrages committed by the Defenders. The Dublin Society reacted by publishing a resolution declaring that the secret committee was unconstitutional. The resolution was signed by Simon Butler, chairman and Oliver Bond, a merchant, as secretary; each was fined £500 and sentenced to six months imprisonment for breach of privilege. At the request of the society, Tone prepared for publication 'An Address to the Nation', protesting against the treatment of Butler and Bond. In true eighteenth century spirit, the society also decided to give a series of splendid dinners within the walls of Newgate Prison, to honour the two martyrs.

Thomas Russell was summoned by the secret committee to give evidence and he was questioned about Tone's letter to him (pp. 16–17). He wondered how they had got hold of it, and wrote in his diary for 20 March 1793, 'I gave it to Digges so that he could copy it. Surely he could not have been so base?'[10] The committee got little out of Russell. He refused to give evidence on oath about other people's opinions and would not answer any question if it seemed to him that his answer might put someone else in danger.

The Catholic Convention sat again in April 1793 and the general mood was that they should accept the reliefs obtained as a big step forward and, by resolution, thank all those who had contributed to securing them. The King and Hobart were duly thanked in formal fashion. Their appreciation of Tone's work was shown in a more tangible way; he was voted

£1,500, together with a medal, suitably inscribed, value thirty guineas. Smaller sums were voted to Simon Butler and Todd Jones. In the event, funds ran short, and only Tone and Butler received any money. Tone was paid in instalments over a long period.

The Catholic Committee then decided to wind up the convention, but as a last step, they passed a resolution in favour of parliamentary reform. This was done principally to show their gratitude to the Belfast Dissenters for their strong and unwavering support. It proved very unwise, on two counts. First, it took them out of their proper field, Catholic relief, into general politics, and second, it angered the King, George III, and changed his favourable attitude to one of unshakeable opposition to further concessions to the Catholics. Only seven years later, when emancipation seemed well nigh assured as part of the bargaining about the Act of Union, the King objected, convinced that to grant it would be a breach of his coronation oath to uphold a Protestant constitution, and Pitt was obliged to resign, as he could not carry out his undertaking.

The resolution also gave Fitzgibbon an opportunity to show Pitt how untrustworthy the Catholics were, and how great a danger they could be to the established order. On 14 May 1793, he wrote to Pitt:

Lord Westmoreland has, I presume, apprised you of the proceedings of the Catholic Convention at their last meeting — that they declared their intention to unite their efforts with the friends of parliamentary reform, and voted to Mr Butler the precise sum in which he had been fined for libelling the House of Lords. However strongly these circumstances mark their disposition towards the established government, one other vote of money they passed will, I hope, explain to you fully and unequivocally that I am not mistaken in the opinion which I submitted to you that their ultimate object is to separate this country from Great Britain.

They have voted £1,500 to a Mr Tone, who is their Cabinet minister and adviser, who first proposed an alliance between Puritans and Catholics, and whose great object will be explained to you by the paper [Tone's letter to Russell] which I have the honour to enclose to you much better than by any comment of mine on the subject. This gentleman has been called to our Bar. He is the son of a bankrupt tradesman and has the merit of being the founder of the Society of United Irishmen. He was also the original projector of the Catholic Convention ... and composed most of the seditious and treasonable libels which are put forth by the Society of United Irishmen. The paper which I enclose to you is also one of his composition. It was written early in the summer of 1791 and privately circulated by him amongst his confidential friends in Dublin and Belfast. The first part of it contains the first Declaration of the Society of United Irishmen and was printed and distributed by them on their first formation. The latter part, you will see, contains his private opinion of the means necessary to be pursued to carry the main object.

This gentleman at present is the confidential agent and adviser of the men who govern the whole body of the Roman Catholics. They have already paid him very large sums of money and concluded their last sitting by voting him a further sum of £1,500.

Mr Tone is also a very great friend and intimate of a young gentleman whose name I mentioned to you very lately whose connexions certainly ought to guard him against such a companion.

I have the honour to be, my dear Sir, with great

truth and respect, your faithful and most humble servant, Fitzgibbon.[11]

The young gentleman referred to was most probably George Knox. This letter is both inaccurate and biased. Tone was not the original projector of the Catholic Convention nor had he been paid large sums of money by the Catholics.

Fitzgibbon used Tone's letter to push the Convention Bill through parliament. His speech in the debate drew a long and vehement reply from Tone in a letter addressed to the editor of *Faulkner's Journal* referring to the report of Fitzgibbon's speech in the issue of 11 July 1793.[12] 'The charge against me', wrote Tone, 'is, that I am one of a faction, whose object is, in the words of the speech, "to rebel against the crown of Great Britain, by effectuating a separation between the sister countries". And the overt acts which are brought forward to establish the charge, are a letter, or confidential despatch, said to be written by me: the founding of the society of United Irishmen; the establishing the General Committee of the Catholics, on a plan, procured from my friends and associates in France.' He went on to deal with the charge that he advocated separation from England. A connection between the two countries would be beneficial to both only if it were one of perfect equality, equal law, equal commerce, equal liberty, equal justice. The existing abuses and corruption, and the despair he felt of ever seeing them removed, first brought him to think of the idea of separation. He did not regard the mention of separation as either treason or blasphemy. Turning to his letter of July 1791, he pointed out that by substituting 'we' for 'I', Fitzgibbon tried to convey that Tone was involved in a conspiracy. Further, Fitzgibbon alleged that Tone 'struck out for the Catholics that plan of election which he received from his friends and associates in France.' This Tone

denied categorically. 'It is the only misfortune of a
free government that nothing but full and legal proof
can bring such dark conspirators to condign punishment,' said Fitzgibbon, a remark to chill the blood of
anyone who believed in justice and freedom. 'Alas!
Alas!' was Tone's comment. 'The cruel lenity of the
law which again intervenes and ties up the hands of
this friend to rational liberty.'

The core of Tone's thinking on the connection
with England and on the breaking of that connection,
may be found earlier in his letter to *Faulkner's Journal*. 'I beg leave to protest solemnly against the principle laid down by the writer that, as an Irishman, I
owe any allegiance either to Great Britain or to the
crown of Great Britain. My allegiance is due to the
King of Ireland; and I would, to the last drop of my
blood, resist the claim of any king, and much more of
any nation, under any other title, who should presume
to exact obedience of me.'

Tone's fourth child was born that year, 1793, and
was named Francis Rawdon, after Lord Rawdon, his
godfather. Rawdon, who was now Lord Moira, having
succeeded his father, was entertained by the Catholics
at a banquet in Dublin, in recognition of the help he
had given them in London in January 1793. The toasts
were drafted by Tone and Keogh and made no mention of either the Northern Dissenters or the United
Irishmen. The society seemed to have lost its initial
momentum and membership had fallen off. This was
probably due to a combination of circumstances: the
concentration of public interest on the fight by the
Catholics for civil and political rights, alarm at the
mounting scale of agrarian outrages perpetrated by
Defenders, and the outbreak of war with France.

Now Tone, like Othello, found that his occupation
was gone. With great reluctance, he began to prepare
himself to return to practice at the Bar.

4
The Jackson Affair and Exile to America

Some time in 1791, Tone had gone into possession of
a cottage in Co. Kildare. It was on the estate of the
Wolfes of Blackhall, and probably a gift or extended
loan from them, as he was in no position to pay for
any property. It had a tower at one end and Tone, as
ever given to playful nicknames, called it the 'Chateau
Boue'.

It seems that he spent the latter half of 1793 at
this country cottage. Russell had by that time resigned
his post in Dungannon, and his diary records a visit to
'Mr Hutton at his seat in the country', on Sunday, 1
December 1793. The following Tuesday, 3 December,
the anniversary of the Catholic Convention, he dined
at Magog's (Richard McCormick), and found 'that
nothing in a political way is doing; all talking.' Later,
he wrote, 'Everything is going from bad to worse!
The French, establishing their liberty, would free us
in our own despite. Down to Chateau Boue. Mr Hutton determines to go to the Bar.'[13]

The Jackson affair ended this period of stagnation.
Unfortunately, Tone's Journals for this period have
been lost, but he wrote a full account of his involvement in the affair in the form of a memorandum.

The central figure in the episode, the Rev. William
Jackson, was a clergyman of the Church of England,
which has harboured many bizarre clerics but none
stranger than Jackson. He was born in Dublin about
1737 and educated at Oxford. He became a curate in

London, and then secretary to the notorious Elizabeth [42] Chudleigh. She was a maid of honour to the Princess of Wales, and at twenty-four married the Honourable Augustus Hervey, a lieutenant in the navy. As they were both poor, and she did not wish to lose her post as maid of honour, the marriage was kept secret. Her conduct was the talk of London, even in that age of scandal. In 1749, five years after her marriage, she appeared as Iphigenia at a masked ball, naked save for a diaphanous gauze dress. Later she became mistress to the Duke of Kingston, married him after ten years, and was tried for bigamy after he died in 1773, leaving her his immense fortune. The House of Lords found her guilty, but she escaped the punishment of being burnt on the hand by pleading the privilege of her peerage.

Jackson's connection with her began some time before her trial. He left the Church, went into journalism and edited the *Public Ledger,* a daily paper. Soon after her trial, he accompanied the Duchess to France, spent some years there, and on his return to London became editor of the *Morning Post.* In France he had imbibed revolutionary ideas, and made the acquaintance of an Irishman named Nicholas Madgett, an official in the French Ministry of Foreign Affairs. He was now commissioned by Madgett to find out the chances of success for a French invasion of England or Ireland. In London he renewed a friendship with one Cockayne, a former attorney to Elizabeth Chudleigh. Cockayne instantly betrayed him to Pitt, and then undertook to accompany him to Ireland and report his activities, in return for a pension and payment of debts. They arrived in Dublin on 1 April 1794 and were met by a friend of both, Leonard McNally, barrister and United Irishman. McNally became probably the most successful spy ever employed by the British government in Ireland. He defended Tone,

Emmet, Tandy and other leaders in court, fought a duel with Sir Jonah Barrington in defence of the [43] honour of the United Irishmen, was deep in their councils while all the time informing on them, and died, still unsuspected, twenty-two years after the Rising of 1798.

McNally arranged that Jackson and Cockayne should be introduced to Hamilton Rowan, then in Newgate Jail serving a two-year sentence for sedition. Rowan agreed to assist them, and suggested that Tone might prepare a memorandum on the state of Ireland. After several meetings with Rowan, Jackson and Cockayne, Tone drew up a paper, the general tenor of which was that circumstances in Ireland were favourable to a French invasion, and adding that a force of not less than 10,000 would ensure success. At a further meeting in Rowan's room in Newgate, (it must be remembered that in those days prisoners with sufficient means were allowed to make themselves quite comfortable in jail, with ample accommodation and freedom to receive visitors privately) Tone gave his paper to Jackson, but a few minutes later, realising that he knew very little about this stranger, he took it back before Jackson could read it, and gave it to Rowan, saying that he might copy it but should then burn the original. About a week later, Tone was extremely vexed and alarmed when Rowan told him that he had given two or three copies, with several alterations, to Jackson, and had burnt the original, as Tone had asked. He determined, he says, to withdraw himself as soon as he could from a business wherein he saw such grievous indiscretion. The question was raised of a suitable person to travel to France to put the case for an invasion at first-hand to the Committee of Public Safety. It seems that the others were unanimous that no better or more suitable emissary than Tone could be found. Tone demurred, saying that he was a man of no fortune, with a wife and children dependent on him and that his going to France was completely out of the question. It is probable that he also realised that the considerable sums due to him from the Catholic Committee might never be received if he left the country.

Tone had undoubtedly compromised himself to a perilous degree by his meetings with an avowed agent of revolutionary France, then at war with England, and by his paper encouraging the French to pursue the idea of an invasion of Ireland. The danger of their position was made very clear to both himself and Rowan when Jackson was arrested on 28 April. It was at this point that McNally turned informer to save himself. Rowan managed to escape from Newgate on 1 May and made his way to France on a fishing vessel. Tone had his wife and family to consider. Realising that, in his own words, his situation was a very critical one, he sought the advice and assistance of his aristocratic friends, George Knox and Marcus Beresford, Member of Parliament and son of the powerful John Beresford. There was another friend in a high place, the Attorney-General, later Lord Kilwarden, a cousin of the Theobald Wolfe after whom he had been named. With the help of these friends, an agreement or compromise was reached. Tone agreed to emigrate to America and the authorities undertook that no action would be taken against him nor would he be called as a witness in the trial of Jackson.

Tone has left an account of an interview he had with 'a gentleman high in confidence with the administration' at which the compromise was arranged. He admitted that his conduct had placed him at the mercy of the government but said that he would not fly the country, nor would he appear as a witness against either Rowan or Jackson. He was prepared to go to America as soon as he could arrange his affairs. The gentleman, after a short time, assured him that he should not be attacked as a principal, nor summoned as a witness. Tone goes on, 'Whether this, which is the whole of the communication between government and me, is a compromise or not, I hope, at least, it is no dishonourable one. I have betrayed no friend: I have revealed no secret: I have abused no confidence.'

As part of the agreement, Tone prepared a full account of his dealings with Jackson. The penultimate paragraph reads: 'I have framed the foregoing narrative, relying implicitly on the honour of the gentlemen to whom I willingly confide it, that no use whatsoever shall be made of it against any one of the parties concerned in any judicial transaction: I give it for political purposes only.'

The trial of Jackson did not take place until April 1795, a year after his meetings with Tone and Rowan. The defence had difficulties in preparing their case, and the prosecution had their own difficulties with their principal witness, Cockayne. As a counter-agent, he was as incompetent as the man he was spying on, and seems to have spent his time in Dublin in a state of misery and fear. In letters to Pitt, he complained that Jackson would not let him go to bed before two in the morning or without having at least three bottles of claret, whereas a pint of wine was his usual stint, adding pathetically, 'besides, the expense is enormous.'[14] Before the arrest of Jackson, Cockayne suggested to Pitt that Tone was 'a man of ten times more consequence to Ireland than Jackson, and on him will be found in all likelihood letters from Rowan to some persons in the executive government of France, as also some letters from Jackson.'

The Irish government, for reasons that will be discussed later, decided to arrest Jackson and to deal with Tone in another way. Two days after the arrest, Cockayne revealed his terror at his own situation in a further letter to Pitt: 'I depended on you to protect [46] me from the disgrace of a common informer...the steps the government of Ireland have taken with me have so far degraded me as to make me loathe my existence and instead of here finding a generous shelter for me, they are anxious to bring me forward into a situation that my life is in the most immediate danger, my character for ever blasted, and I had better been the tacit spectator of my country's fall than ever in the least interfered therein.'[15]

With Jackson in jail, Rowan in France, a compromise arranged with Tone, and Cockayne, in terror for his life, anxious to keep well in the background, a curious lull now came over the affair, while Jackson awaited trial. The lull was more apparent than real. The Irish government took swift action against the United Irishmen, raided their premises and seized their papers, to the great indignation of Dr Drennan, who blamed the members who had been involved with Jackson, namely, Tone and Rowan, for drawing down the government on the society. Until then a quite legal and open reforming society, it was now suppressed and driven underground. This development, and the clear impossibility of achieving any worthwhile reform by constitutional means, turned the United Irishmen towards more direct methods of winning a wider freedom than they had hitherto sought.

The year between Jackson's arrest and his trial was an anxious time for Tone, although he states that he had a letter from the under-secretary, Sackville Hamilton, written to him by order of the Lord Lieutenant, Westmoreland, guaranteeing him from all attack. This did not prevent Ponsonby and other enemies from threatening that he would be implicated. He was re-employed by the Catholic Committee at Christmas 1794, an unwise move on their part. It allowed their inveterate enemy, Lord Chancellor Fitzgibbon, to assert that their employment of an acknowledged United Irishman and a man who had been deeply [47] involved in a treasonable conspiracy showed them in their true colours as enemies of the state.

In not being brought to trial himself, Tone was certainly let off lightly. He had powerful friends, it is true, but even they could scarcely have saved him from Fitzgibbon's enmity if the Lord Chancellor had not seen a balance of advantage to his own designs in allowing Tone to remain at large, and, as it turned out, unwittingly to serve Fitzgibbon's ends by accepting employment from the Catholics, thus compromising them.

At this stage there occurred a political change in England which had a decisive influence on the course of events in Ireland. To strengthen his weakening administration, Pitt arranged a merger with elements of the Whig opposition, which joined the government. Lord Fitzwilliam, who was related to the Ponsonbys through his wife, was nominated Lord Lieutenant to replace Westmoreland. He was known to be favourably disposed towards the claims of the Catholics and the news of his appointment was hailed by them. Unfortunately, a delay of several months between the announcement and his taking up office on 4 January 1795, enabled Fitzgibbon and the Beresfords to move to thwart him. Fitzgibbon managed to implant firmly in the mind of George III the idea that to admit Catholics to sit as members of parliament would be a breach of his coronation oath to maintain the Protestant constitution as by law established.

The advent of Fitzwilliam seems to have opened to Tone a prospect of employment by the new administration. This was unfounded optimism. Tone was by nature sanguine, and it was not unnatural that a man in his vulnerable and precarious position should grasp at any opportunity. In a memorandum of 7 February

1795, he records that three leading Catholics, Byrne, [48] Hamill and Keogh, waited on Grattan to recommend Tone to the new administration. Tone briefed them particularly on three matters which he thought might prejudice Grattan against him. As to the first, that he was a United Irishman, their reply should be that he never had any influence with them, that they regarded him as using the society to further Catholic claims and that he had had no connection with them since May 1793. The second concerned the formation of a National Guard on the Parisian model. He had had no connection with that, as he had been in London with the petitioners to the King when the Guard was formed. The third was the most serious, his involvement with Jackson. He admitted that he had been most indiscreet, but pleaded that as the Westmoreland administration had not thought he merited punishment, he hoped he would find himself, if not bettered, at least not injured by the change in government.

The approach to Grattan proved fruitless. It must have angered Tone's enemies, for in his Journal of June 1796 he records that it was a million to one then that he would be hanged as a traitor.

The new Lord Lieutenant let it be known that he was firmly committed to full Catholic emancipation and for good measure, dismissed John Beresford, commissioner of the revenue and close friend of Fitzgibbon, whose anti-Catholic views he shared wholeheartedly. This abrupt sacking, intended to clear the way for parliamentary reform, struck at the heart of Castle officialdom. Beresford had a host of relations in positions of power and it was a fatal mistake on Fitzwilliam's part. Pitt, while sympathetic to Catholic aspirations, was only too well aware of the entrenched nature of the opposition and had expected Fitzwilliam to move with caution. In addition to his friends in Ireland, Beresford had powerful allies in England. On

19 February 1795, six weeks after he had arrived in Dublin, the British government decided to recall Fitz- [49] william.

The Catholics made a desperate attempt to save the situation and even to avert the recall of Fitzwilliam, by sending a deputation to London in February 1795. Again, Tone accompanied them as secretary. Their efforts failed utterly and they returned to Dublin in deep despondency.

Jackson came up for trial on 23 April 1795, and was defended by John Philpot Curran, George Ponsonby and McNally. Curran's cross-examination of the wretched Cockayne was devastating and he tore the spy's character to shreds. He was a bad witness, but his evidence was sufficient, together with the documents seized by the Crown, or given to them by him, to secure a conviction. Jackson was brought up for sentence on 30 April, and became unconscious in the dock. A doctor was called and declared he was dying. A few minutes later he was pronounced dead. At an inquest the next day, a surgeon found that Jackson's stomach contained a metallic poison. His wife had visited him before he came to court and it was assumed that she had brought the poison.

During the trial, Tone made it a point to show himself openly in Dublin so that it could not be said that he had stolen away secretly. His name was mentioned more than once in court, and those not aware of his compromise with the government must have wondered why he, too, was not arraigned. He resolved not to embarass his friends by calling on them. Nevertheless, the occasion of his leaving Ireland, as it might be for ever, drew forth heart-warming displays of support and sympathy from many friends.

'A short time before my departure', he wrote, 'my friend Russell being in town, he and I walked out together, to Rathfarnham, to see Emmet, who has a charming villa there. He showed us a little study, of [50] an elliptical form, which he was building at the bottom of the lawn, and which he said he would consecrate to our meetings, if ever we lived to see our country emancipated. I begged of him, if he intended Russell should be of the party, in addition to the books and maps it would naturally contain, to fit up a small cellaret, which should contain a few dozen of his best old claret. He showed me that he had not omitted that circumstance, which he acknowledged to be essential, and we both rallied Russell with considerable success. I mention this trifling anecdote because I love the men, and because it seems now, at least possible, that we may yet meet again in Emmet's study. As we walked together into town, I opened my plan to them both. I told them that I considered my compromise with government to extend no further than the banks of the Delaware, and that the moment I landed, I was free to follow any plan which might suggest itself to me, for the emancipation of my country; that, undoubtedly, I was guilty of a great offence against the existing government; that, in consequence, I was going into exile; and that I considered that exile as a full expiation for the offence; and consequently, felt myself at liberty, having made that sacrifice, to begin again on a fresh score. They both agreed with me on those principles, and I then proceeded to tell them that my intention was, immediately on my arrival in Philadelphia, to wait on the French Minister to detail to him, fully, the situation of affairs in Ireland, to endeavour to obtain a recommendation to the French government, and, if I succeeded so far, to leave my family in America, and to set off instantly for Paris, and apply, in the name of my country, for the assistance of France, to enable us to assert our independence. It is unnecessary, I believe, to say, that this plan met with the warmest approbation and support from both Russell and Emmet; we shook hands, and, having repeated our professions of unalterable regard [51] and esteem for each other, we parted!'

At a meeting of the Catholics of the city of Dublin on 9 April 1795, it was resolved unanimously that

> the thanks of the meeting be respectfully presented to their agent, Theobald Wolfe Tone, for the readiness with which he accompanied their deputies to England, and the many other important services rendered the Catholic body — services which no gratitude could overrate, and no remuneration overpay.

McCormick and Keogh, of the Catholic Committee, called on him and fully approved his plan. Tone was astonished that the government permitted him to go to Philadelphia, knowing that there was a French Minister there, without exacting an assurance that he would have no communication with him. George Knox sent him a parcel of books, to while away the voyage, and asked particularly for an address in America to which he might write, adding significantly 'as any letters directed immediately to you, will certainly not get unopened through the post office'.

On 20 May 1795, Tone set out for Belfast with his wife, his sister Mary and his three children (the second had died very young). His whole property, he said, consisted of their clothes, his books and about £700 in money and bills on Philadelphia.

'If our friends in Dublin were kind and affectionate, those in Belfast, if possible, were still more so', he wrote. 'Even those who scarcely knew me were eager to entertain: parties and excursions were planned for our amusement. . . . I remember particularly two days that we passed on the Cave Hill. On the first Russell, Neilson, Simms, McCracken and one or two more of us, on the summit of McArt's fort, took a solemn

obligation — which I think I may say I have on my part
[52] endeavoured to fulfil — never to desist in our efforts
until we had subverted the authority of England over
our country and asserted her independence.

'Another day we had the tent of the first regiment
pitched in the Deer Park, and a company of thirty of
us, including the family of the Simms, Neilson's,
McCracken's and my own, dined and spent the day
together deliciously.'

On 15 June 1795, they embarked on board the
Cincinnatus, of Wilmington. Their friends in Belfast
filled their cabin with sea stores, fresh provisions,
sweetmeats and everything they could think of for
the comfort of the family. Before their departure,
Tone explained to Simms, Neilson and Charles G.
Teeling (a leader in the Defenders), his intention of
looking for French aid through the Minister in Philadelphia and received their complete approval. 'I now
looked upon myself', he wrote 'as competent to speak
fully and with confidence for the Catholics, for the
Dissenters and for the Defenders of Ireland.'

Tone has left a vivid account of the passage to
America in the *Cincinnatus.*

We were now at sea, and at leisure to examine
our situation. I had hired a state room, which was
about eight feet by six, in which we had fitted up
three berths; my wife and our youngest little boy
occupied one, my sister and my little girl the
second, and our eldest boy and myself the third. It
was at first grievously inconvenient, but necessity
and custom by degrees reconciled us to our situation; our greatest suffering was want of good
water, under which we laboured the whole passage,
and which we found it impossible to replace by
wine, porter, or spirits, of which we had abundance. The captain was tolerably civil, the vessel was

stout, and we had good weather almost the whole of our voyage. But we had 300 passengers on board [53] of a ship of 250 tons, and of course crowded to a degree not to be conceived by those who have not been on board a passenger ship. The slaves who are carried from the coast of Africa have much more room allowed them than the miserable emigrants who pass from Ireland to America; for the avarice of the captains in that trade is such, that they think they can never load their vessels sufficiently, and they trouble their heads in general no more about the accommodation and stowage of their passengers, than of any other lumber aboard. I laboured, and with some success, to introduce something like a police, and to a certain degree, though a very imperfect one, of cleanliness among them. Certainly, the air of the sea must be wonderfully wholesome; for, if the same number of wretches of us had been shut up in the same space ashore, with so much inconvenience of every kind about us, two-thirds of us would have died in the time of our voyage. As it was, in spite of everything, we were tolerably healthy; we lost but one passenger, a woman; we had some sick aboard, and the friendship of James MacDonnell, of Belfast, having supplied me with a small medicine chest and written directions, I took on myself the office of physician. I prescribed and administered accordingly, and I had the satisfaction to land all my patients safe and sound.... Thirty days of our voyage had now passed over without any event, save the ordinary ones of seeing now a shoal of porpoises, now a shark, now a set of dolphins, the peacocks of the sea, playing about, and once or twice a whale.... At length, abut the 20th of July, some time after we had cleared the banks of Newfoundland, we were stopped by three British frigates, the

Thetis, Captain Lord Cochrane, the *Hussar,* Captain [54] Rose, and the *Esperance,* Captain Wood, who boarded us, and after treating us with the greatest insolence, both officers and sailors, they pressed every one of our hands, save one, and near fifty of my unfortunate fellow passengers, who were most of them flying to America to avoid the tyranny of a bad government at home, and who had thus most unexpectedly, fell under the severest tyranny, one of them, at least, which exists. As I was in jacket and trousers, one of the lieutenants ordered me into the boat, as a fit man to serve the king, and it was only the screams of my wife and sister which induced him to desist. It would have been a pretty termination to my adventures if I had been pressed and sent aboard a man of war. The insolence of these tyrants, as well to myself as to my poor fellow passengers, in whose fate a fellowship in misfortune had interested me, I have not since forgotten, and I never will. At length, after detaining us two days, during which they rummaged us at least twenty times, they suffered us to proceed.

On the 30th July, we made Cape Henlopen; the 31st we ran up the Delaware, and the 1st of August we landed safe at Wilmington, not one of us providentially having been for an hour indisposed on the passage, nor even sea sick. Those only who have had their wives, their children, and all, in short, that is dear to them, floating for seven or eight weeks at the mercy of the winds and waves, can conceive the transport I felt at seeing my wife and our darling babies ashore once again in health and in safety. We set up at the principal tavern, kept by an Irishman, one Captain O'Byrne O'Flynn, (I think), for all the taverns in America are kept by majors and captains, either of the militia or continentals, and in a few days we had entirely recruited our strength and spirits, and totally forgotten the fatigues of the voyage.

About the 7th or 8th of August, Tone went on to Philadelphia, where he found an old friend, Dr Reynolds, chairman of the Dublin United Irishmen at the time of the Jackson affair, who had fled on the arrest of Jackson. Hamilton Rowan had arrived from France six weeks previously and the three men met that evening. In Paris, Rowan had submitted memorials on the state of Ireland to the Committee of Public Safety. These were received with interest, but on 9 Thermidor (27 July) 1794 Robespierre fell from power and was guillotined the following day. In the political turmoil that followed, Rowan and his memorials were completely forgotten. After kicking his heels in Paris for a few months, he sailed for America.

Tone told them of his plans and Rowan gave him a letter of introduction to the French Minister, Citizen Adet, whom he had known in Paris. The meeting with Adet was disappointing. Tone gave him his only credentials, two votes of thanks from the Catholics, and his certificate of admission into the Belfast Volunteers. His difficulties were not lessened when he found that the Minister spoke poor English, and he admitted ruefully that his own French was worse. Adet asked for a memorial on the situation in Ireland. Tone produced this in a few days, though almost prostrated by the extreme heat, the temperature varying between 90 and 97 degrees. He offered to go to France on the first vessel available but the Minister would not hear of this, pointing out the danger of capture by the British navy. He did undertake to forward the memorial to the French government with his strongest recommendations. Tone was downcast. 'It was barely possible, but I did not much expect that the French government might take notice of my memorial, and if they did not, there was an end to all my hopes'.

He now resigned himself to settling in America, and began to look around for a suitable farm. His heart was heavy at the prospect, as is revealed in long letters to his closest friend, Thomas Russell.[16] He disliked intensely the Americans he saw in Philadelphia. 'They seem a selfish, churlish, unsocial race, totally absorbed in making money; a mongrel breed, half English, half Dutch, with the worst qualities of both countries.'

The want of Russell's company was a constant pang.

Believe me, dear Tom, the greatest of the numberless heavy losses I sustained in leaving Ireland, and especially in leaving Belfast, my adopted mother, was the loss of your society; and I speak for us all. There does not a day elapse that we do not speak of you, nor a ridiculous or absurd idea or circumstance arise that we do not regret that you are not with us to share and enjoy it with us. You know how exactly our humours concurred, and that particular style of conversation which we had framed for ourselves and which was to us so exquisitely pleasant; those strained quotations, absurd phrases and extravagant sallies which people in the unreserve of affectionate intercourse indulge themselves in — all these we yet enjoy, but woefully curtailed by your absence. If anything brighter than ordinary occurs, the first idea is 'Ah, poor Tom! I wish he was here with us now!' It is a selfish wish; never come here unless you are driven. Stick to your country to the last plank, as I would have done had I been able; much as I regret your absence, I cannot in conscience wish you were with us. You and I have known Ireland. . . .

Tone finally decided to settle in Princeton, New Jersey, and agreed with a Captain Leonard to buy a [57] plantation of 180 acres, half under timber, for £1,180.[17] He moved his family to Princeton and rented a small house for the winter. 'I fitted up my study and began to think my lot was cast to be an American farmer.'

In another long letter to Russell, he wrote 'You held that all countries were alike to a well regulated mind. I do not wish you so ill as to desire you to be convinced of the contrary by such an experiment as I am now making, but, if it ever should be your lot, I believe you will feel the irresistible affection by which a man is drawn to his native soil, and how flat and uninteresting the politics and parties of other countries appear.'

He dwelt again on the repugnance he felt towards the settlers he had met.

In the country parts of Pennsylvania the farmers are extremely ignorant and boorish — particularly the Germans and their descendants, who abound. There is something, too, in the Quaker manners extremely unfavourable to anything like polished society. But of all the people I have met here the Irish are incontestably the most offensive. If you meet a confirmed blackguard, you may be sure he is Irish; you will, of course, observe I speak of the lower orders. They are as boorish and ignorant as the Germans, as uncivil and uncouth as the Quakers, and, as they have ten times more animal spirits than both, they are much more actively troublesome. After all, I do not wonder at, nor am I angry with them. They are corrupted by their own execrable government at home; and when they land here and find themselves treated like human creatures — fed and clothed and paid for their labours, no longer flying from the sight of any fellow who is able to purchase a velvet collar to his coat — I do not wonder if the heads of the unfortunate devils are turned with such an unexpected change in their fortunes, and if their new-gotten liberty breaks out, as it too often does, into pettiness and insolence. For all this it is perhaps not fair to blame them; the fact is certain. In Jersey the manners of the people are extremely different; they seem lively and disengaged in comparison, and that among others was one reason which determined me to settle in this State. But, if the manners of the Pennsylvanians be unpleasant, their government is the best under heaven and their country thrives accordingly. You can have no idea, from anything you have ever seen or read or fancied, of the affluence and ease in which they universally live, and, as to the want of civility, they do not feel it.

Looking ahead, Tone and his wife became anguished at the thought of their children's future. To what purpose would they give them an education which would only tend to make them discontented with their situation and surroundings? Their daughter caused them keen anxiety. 'How could we bear to see her the wife of a clown without delicacy or refinement?'[18]

So Tone passed several months in the deepest despondency while waiting for his lawyer to prepare the deeds for his purchase. Towards the end of November 1795, he was roused from this state of near despair by the receipt of letters from Keogh, Russell and the two Simms. They carried the message that 'the state of the public mind in Ireland was advancing to republicanism faster than even he could believe.' They pressed him to fulfil his promise to them at his departure and to move heaven and earth to force his way to the French government to seek its

assistance. Simms authorised him to draw on him for
£200 sterling towards his expenses.

Tone showed the letters to his wife and sister.
Courageously, they both urged him to do as his friends
had asked. He immediately set off for Philadelphia to
see the French Minister again, and showed him the
letters from Ireland. Citizen's Adet's reception of him
this time was most encouraging. He offered to write
to the French government recommending Tone in the
strongest way and also offered Tone money for his
expenses. Tone gratefully accepted the offer of letters
of recommendation but declined to take any money.
He then sent for his youngest brother, Arthur, aged
thirteen or fourteen, who was at Princeton, and put
him on board the *Susanna,* bound for Belfast, which
sailed from Philadelphia on 10 December 1795. He
told Arthur of his plan to sail to France at the first
opportunity and instructed him to inform Neilson,
Simms and Russell of this immediately on his arrival
in Belfast. He was then to go to Dublin and inform
Keogh and McCormick. Everyone else, including his
father and mother, was to be told that Theobald had
purchased a farm in Princeton and settled there.

Having despatched him, I settled all my affairs
as speedily as possible. I drew on Simms for £200,
agreeable to his letter, £150 sterling of which I
devoted to my voyage; my friend Reynolds procured me *louis d'or* at the bank for £100 sterling
worth of silver. I converted the remainder of my
little property into bank stock, and, having signed
a general power of attorney to my wife, I waited
finally on Adet, who gave me a letter in cypher
directed to the *Comité de Salut Public,* the only
credential which I intended to bring with me to
France. I spent one day in Philadelphia with Reynolds, Rowan and my old friend and fellow suf-

ferer, James Napper Tandy, who, after a long concealment and many adventures, was recently arrived from Hamburg, and at length on the 13th December, at night, I arived at Princeton, whither Rowan accompanied me, bringing with me a few presents for my wife, sister, and our dear little babies. That night we supped together in high spirits, and Rowan retiring immediately after, my wife, sister and I sat together till very late engaged in that kind of animated and enthusiastic conversation which our characters and the nature of the enterprise I was embarked in may be supposed to give rise to. The courage and firmness of the women supported me, and them too, beyond my expectations; we had neither tears nor lamentations but, on the contrary, the most ardent hope and the most steady resolution.

Tone arrived in New York on 16 December and booked his passage on the *Jersey*, using the alias 'James Smith' as a precaution. He remained in New York for ten days and while there received a letter from his wife, informing him that she was with child, 'a circumstance which she had concealed so far, I am sure, lest it might have had some influence on my determination.' Nothing more is heard of this child; it may have been stillborn, or the pregnancy may have been terminated by a miscarriage. His narrative continues:

On the 1st January 1796, I sailed from Sandy Hook, with nine fellow passengers, bound for Havre de Grace. Our voyage lasted exactly one month, during the most part of which we had heavy blowing weather: five times we had such gales of wind as obliged us to lie under a close reefed mizen stay-sail; however, our ship was stout. We had plenty of provisions, wine, brandy and especially, what I thought more of, remembering my last voyage, excellent water, so that I had no reason to com- plain of my passage. We did not meet a single vessel of force, either French or English; we passed three or four Americans, bound mostly, like ourselves, to France. On the 27th we were in soundings, at 85 fathoms; on the 28th we made the Lizard, and at length, on the 1st February, we landed in safety at Havre de Grace, having met with not the smallest accident during our voyage.

5
Mission in France

'Wolfe Tone was a most extraordinary man and his history is the most curious history of those times. With a hundred guineas in his pocket, unknown and unrecommended, he went to Paris in order to overturn the British government in Ireland. He asked for a large force, Lord Edward Fitzgerald for a small one. They listened to Tone....'

So wrote the Duke of Wellington, renowned for his sagacity and his penetrating common sense. When Tone landed at Le Havre de Notre Dame de Grace, which he called Havre de Grace, and which is now styled Le Havre, he was, as usual, full of hope of success in his undertaking. But many weary and frustrating days were to pass after his landing on 1 February 1796 before the French authorities listened to him and acted.

In Havre he lodged at the Hotel de Paix and revelled in the luxury of 'a superb damask bed, after being a month without having my clothes off'. His Journal for the period from his landing in France until June 1798, a few months before he was captured in Lough Swilly, has survived and gives a lively account of France in the early years of the Revolution.

The day after his arrival he walked around the town, which he found ugly and dirty. It was a weekday, but Mass was being celebrated in the church with a good attendance. English propaganda had represented the French as starving, and by way of ironical comment, Tone gives his dinner menu: an excellent soup, a dish of fish fresh from the harbour, a fore- quarter of delicate small mutton, like the Welsh; a superb turkey and a pair of ducks roasted; pastry, cheese and fruit after dinner, with wine *ad libitum,* 'very glad to see such unequivocal proofs of famine.' In the evening he went to the theatre. The house was full and the audience, which included several fine-looking officers, was just as gay 'as if there were no such thing as war and brown bread'.

Tone found everything very cheap, because of the depreciation of the French currency against sterling, which was two hundred times its former value in livres and still rising. He paid only the equivalent of twenty-five pence a day for full board and lodging, although he was staying at the best hotel, and his seat at the theatre cost him only fourpence.

He stayed in Havre de Grace nine days, waiting to arrange a conveyance to Paris, and went to the theatre every evening. The *Marseillaise* was sung at each performance and the verse *Tremblez Tyrans* was always received with applause. The behaviour of the young men was extremely decorous and proper. The women were ugly and some wore grotesque head-dresses. The servants at the hotel were remarkably civil and attentive 'which I mention, because I have been so often tormented with blockheads arguing against liberty and equality as subversive of all subordination'.

At length he succeeded in arranging to travel to Paris in a hired coach with a fellow-passenger from America, a Monsieur D'Aucourt. An American, and a doubtful character whom he calls a swindler, took the remaining two places in the coach. Tone lamented his lack of French which obliged him to put up with D'Aucourt, an uncongenial companion, who, he thought, would be indispensable to him in Paris. 'Poor P. P. [Russell]. I shall never meet with such another agreeable companion in a post-chaise. Well, hang sorrow! But I am dreadfully low spirited. . . . I do not bear the separation from my family well.'

[64]

They stayed a night at Rouen and another at Magny, reaching Paris on 12 February 1796. On the journey, Tone noted 'an uninterrupted succession of corn, vines and orchards as far as the eye can reach, rich and *riant* beyond description. I see now clearly that John Bull will be able to starve France.' In fact, Tone deceived himself. Only eighteen months before, France had been saved from near starvation by the arrival of a great convoy of one hundred and thirty grain ships from America. British sea power had ruined French trade. In 1799 there was not a single French merchant ship at sea. Inns might have well-stocked larders, but the poor queued for bread in the cities.

In Paris he stayed at the Hotel des Etrangers, Rue Vivienne, ' a magnificent house, but I foresee as dear as the devil. . . . I must get into private lodgings.' 'As dear as the devil' meant about two guineas a month. That night, his first in Paris, he dined with D'Aucourt at the Restaurateurs in the Maison Egalité, formerly the Palais Royal. They had soup, roast fowl, fried carp, salads of two kinds, a bottle of Burgundy, coffee after dinner and a glass of liqueur, with bread, cauliflower and sauce, all for the equivalent of 4s/7d (23p) sterling. 'What would I have given to have had P. P. with me! Indeed, we would have discussed another bottle of the Burgundy, or by'r Lady, some two or three. . . . The saloon we dined in was magnificent . . . the company of a fashionable appearance . . . everything wore a complete appearance of opulence and luxury.'

After a council of war with D'Aucourt, it was agreed that they should lie low for a day or two, until they got some French clothes made, and then he should call on Monroe, the American Ambassador.

The following evening he went to the Grand Opera and was enchanted by a performance of a ballet, [65] *L'Offrande à la Liberté*. Towards the end, the *Marseillaise* was sung and

> at the words 'Aux armes, citoyens', the stage was filled with National Guards, who rushed in with bayonets fixed, their sabres drawn and their tricolour flag flying. It would be impossible to describe the effect of this. I never knew what enthusiasm was before, and what heightened it beyond all conception was that the men I saw before me were not hirelings, acting a part; they were what they seemed, French citizens flying to arms, to rescue their country from slavery. They were the men who had precipitated Coburg into the Sambre and driven Charlait over the Rhine, and were at this very moment on the eve of hurrying to the frontiers, to encounter fresh dangers and gain fresh glory.

On 15 February, Tone called on the American Ambassador, James Monroe, who later became President of the United States and author of the Monroe Doctrine. He was received very politely and delivered his passport, a letter from Hamilton Rowan and a letter in cipher from an unnamed 'B', probably a friend of Monroe's. Monroe directed him to deliver his dispatch to the Ministry of Foreign Affairs. He went to the Ministry, was introduced to the Minister, Charles Delacroix, (father of the painter; Talleyrand was also reputed to have fathered him) and handed him the letter in cipher from Adet, the Minister in Philadelphia. Again he was received with great politeness and returned to his hotel, well satisfied that he had made a promising start to his mission.

He went to the opera again that night. A seat in a box cost a mere sixpence. 'I lose three-fourths of the pleasure I should otherwise feel, for the want of my

dear love, or my friend, P. P., to share it with.' Walk-
ing about the city the next day, he was struck by the
number of military he saw. 'I now perceive the full
import of the expression, "an armed nation", and I
think I know a country that for its extent and population, could produce as many and as fine fellows as
France.'

On 17 February he called again on Delacroix, who
told him that he had placed his letter before the Executive Directory, who considered it of the greatest
importance. Delacroix then gave him a note intro-
ducing him to Nicholas Madgett, the Irish member of
the Ministry staff who had commissioned the unfortunate Jackson to make his disastrous mission to Ireland in April 1794. Madgett spoke French and English
perfectly, the Minister said, and Tone might open his
mind freely to him. Madgett was delighted to see Tone
and invited him to breakfast the next day so that
they could confer at length.

At breakfast, Madgett assured Tone that the government was in earnest about an invasion of Ireland, and
after a long talk, invited Tone to prepare a memorial
for submission to the Directory. Tone presented his
memorial to Madgett on 22 February and found him
'in the Horrors.' It seems that he had been told that
because of the disorganised state of the French navy,
the government would not risk a large fleet and would
send only 2,000 men, with arms for 20,000 and
artillery.

The navy was indeed disorganised. Revolutionary
ideas and naval discipline were uneasy bedfellows.
Many of the officers were regarded by the sailors as
untrustworthy aristocrats. Disturbances had broken
out in the naval yards at Le Havre, Brest, Cherbourg,
Rochefort and Toulon. The administration in Paris
was too far removed from the coast and too ignorant
of naval affairs to take the proper action to restore

order. Many officers emigrated, the standard of discipline fell ever lower and insubordination was rife. This demoralisation in the navy contrasted starkly with the resounding successes being achieved by the Revolutionary armies commanded by young generals like Hoche and Bonaparte, whose origins were far from aristocratic. Commanding a great army successfully in the field certainly demanded military talent of a high order, but the handling of a fleet of ships, often in bad weather and when they must sail in close formation, required in each ship's company, skill and discipline that could be acquired only by long training. The Directory's doubts about the competence of the navy were only too well founded, as events were to show.

Tone argued forcefully against sending a fleet with fewer than 5,000 men, and Madgett promised to try to secure at least that many. They discussed the question of a commander, which Tone rightly regarded as of paramount importance. Madgett said that the Directory could not spare either Pichegru or Jourdan, who had been mentioned by Tone as men of high repute, well known by character in Ireland. As a third choice, Tone put forward the name of Lazare Hoche, who had gained great renown by his overwhelming defeat of an expedition of French emigrés, supported and equipped by England, at Quiberon Bay, Brittany, the previous July. Madgett said that he was sure that Hoche could be secured to lead the proposed invasion.

It was now becoming clear to Tone that it would require all the tenacity, resourcefulness and persuasiveness that he possessed to ensure the sending of the forces necessary for a successful expedition. 'I never wanted the society, assistance, advice, comfort and direction of the said P. P., half so much as at this moment. I have a pretty serious business on my hands, with a grand responsibility, and here I am, alone, in the midst of Paris, without a single soul to advise or [68] consult with and nothing in fact to support me but a good intention. Sad! Sad! Well, hang fear. "Tis but in vain, for soldiers to complain,"' a line he had learnt from Russell.

The next day, 23 February, Tone called again on Madgett to impress on him his (Tone's) assessment of the situation. With 20,000 men, there would be no possibility of resistance for an hour and they should begin with the capital; with 5,000 he would have no doubt of success but then they should expect some fighting and should begin near Belfast; with 2,000 the business would be utterly desperate. He concluded by saying that nevertheless, if they sent but a sergeant and twelve men, he would go.

He then left Madgett, who, he thought, was honest but weak, and went to see Monroe. The American Ambassador had had Tone's letters decoded and had been particularly impressed by that from Hamilton Rowan. His listened to Tone's account of his dealings with Delacroix and Madgett and then advised him to go at once to the Directory and demand an audience. This did not indicate any want of confidence in either the Minister or Madgett, but it was best to go to the fountainhead. Tone questioned whether it was politic to go over the head of the Minister, but Monroe brushed his objections aside and said that Tone might use his name as a guarantee of good faith. He should ask for either Carnot, 'the organiser of victory' or Le Reveilliere Lepaux, both of whom spoke English. It is indicative of the antagonism still harboured by Americans towards England, although they were no longer at war, that Monroe, Ambassador of a neutral power, should go out of his way to help an Irishman in a mission to persuade the French to mount an invasion of Ireland.

Monroe viewed everything French through rose-coloured spectacles. He told Tone that in all the changes that had taken place in France, there was [69] never an abler or purer set of men at the head of affairs as then. The reality was far different. The Directory was, in the main, venal, corrupt and inefficient and its five members quarrelled incessantly among themselves. Carnot is the only one whose reputation has come down untarnished. He was justly hailed as 'the organiser of victory' for the revolutionary armies, victory due in great measure to his ability, his unremitting hard work and his love of France.

Tone's Journal continues: 'February 24. Went at 12 o'clock in a fright to the Luxembourg, conning speeches in execrable French all the way. What shall I say to Carnot? In the palace, an ante-chamber was filled with people waiting to have an audience. Citizen Carnot appeared in the petit costume of white satin with crimson robe, richly embroidered. It is very elegant and resembles almost exactly the draperies of Van Dyck. He went round the room receiving papers and answering those who addressed him.' Tone succeeded in obtaining a private audience as a stranger just arrived from America, wishing to speak to Citizen Carnot on an affair of consequence. Tone began by saying 'in horrible French' that he had been told that Carnot spoke English. 'A little, Sir, but I perceive you speak French, and, if you please, we will converse in that language.' Tone told him that he was an Irishman and could speak for the Catholics of Ireland, numbering three million, and the Dissenters, almost another million. Both Catholics and Dissenters were burning to throw off the yoke of England and were sympathetic to the French nation. They needed an armed force and money. He had given a memorial on the Irish situation to the Minister for Foreign Affairs, but as the matter was of such vital importance, he had thought it his duty to acquaint the Directory, in person, of his mission. He gave Carnot his assumed name, James Smith, also his real name, which Carnot seemed to recognise. He added that Carnot was very well known by reputation in Ireland and that three years before, they knew he could speak English; this did not displease Carnot. Finally, he gave Monroe as a referee, and asked that he might present himself again, to which Carnot answered, 'By all means'.

Tone's spirits soared after this interview. 'I am a pretty fellow to negotiate with the Directory of France, pull down a monarchy and establish a republic; to break a connection of 600 years standing and contract a fresh alliance with another country... Fitzgibbon used to say that I was a viper in the bosom of Ireland.... I am a better Irishman than he and his whole gang of rascals.... Plunket and Magee would not speak to me in Ireland, because I was a republican. Sink or swim, I stand today on as high ground as either of them ... hunted from my own country as a traitor, living obscurely in America as an exile, and received in France, by the Executive Directory, almost as an Ambassador! ... I am as vain as the devil!'

Tone then drafted a second memorial setting out his views on the best means of achieving the aim of freeing Ireland from English rule and how the Directory could help to accomplish this. He gave it to Madgett to translate, as 'in cool blood I can hardly frame a single sentence in French, and both with Carnot and Delacroix, I run on without the least difficulty.... I dare say I give them abundance of bad language, but no matter for that; they understand me and that is the main point.' Madgett was very slow and Tone had to control his impatience as best he might. He dined alone each evening, for D'Aucourt left him very much to himself, which suited him perfectly. His dinner at Beauvilliers cost him half a crown, including a bottle of Burgundy. 'Beauvilliers has a dead bargain of me for water; I do not think I consume a spoonful in a [71] week. A bottle of Burgundy is too much, and I resolve every morning regularly to drink but the half and every evening regularly I break my resolution. I wish I had P. P. to drink the other half and then perhaps I should live more soberly.' To pass the time while waiting on Madgett to finish the translation, he saw the sights of Paris. He admired the Pantheon but thought that the French were in too much of a hurry to fill it. They had already felt obliged to remove two who had fallen from grace, Marat and Mirabeau. The Hotel des Invalides reminded him of the Royal Hospital in Dublin. In the Louvre he admired the works of Van Dyck, Rubens, Rembrandt and Raphael and rhapsodised over the *Magdalen* of Le Brun, which he thought was worth the whole collection. It now scarcely rates a mention in histories of French painting.

On 11 March he had a long and indecisive interview with Delacroix, who had received and read the translations of his two memorials. The Minister emphasised the difficulty of transporting a large force because of the superiority of the English navy. For his part, Tone pointed out that the larger the force, the more likelihood of the people rising in support. Prompt action was essential as the season was advancing. He went on, 'Seriously, I would attempt it with one hundred men. . . . If the men of property will not support us, they must fall: we can support ourselves by the aid of that numerous and respectable class of the community, *the men of no property.*' That evening, he wrote dejectedly, 'On the whole, I do not much glory in this day's conversation. If I have not lost confidence, I certainly have not gained any.'

On 14 March, he went to the Luxembourg Palace again to see Carnot, but this time he was passed on to General Clarke, head of the War Department. Carnot said, 'Here is almost a countryman of yours, who [72] speaks English perfectly. He has the confidence of government; go with him and explain yourself without reserve.' His first conversation with Clarke was somewhat unnerving. Clarke told him that he was an Irishman, had been in Ireland many times and had many relations there. Tone was therefore the more disturbed when Clarke revealed in his questions his ignorance of the situation in Ireland. He inquired whether the aristocracy could not be expected to join in establishing an independent regime, and whether the Catholic clergy would not influence the people against the French. He even mentioned Fitzgibbon as a possible ally. The meeting ended with Clarke promising to study Tone's two memorials carefully and an agreement that they should meet again in six days time.

It had emerged that Clarke did not know Madgett and this also upset Tone. Was he being fobbed off with subordinates? If he went over their heads, he risked making enemies. He felt keenly the lack of a reliable source of advice. 'This comes of being a stranger. I must grope my way here as well as I can.' He found out, too, that his memorials had not yet reached the Directory.

The memorials make interesting reading. In his first, Tone set down the situation in Ireland, as it appeared to him. He began by pointing out the value of Ireland to England, as a source of food and as a recruiting ground, especially for her navy. Two-thirds of the English navy were Irishmen. He went on to state that the population of Ireland was divided into three religious sects, Protestants, Dissenters and Catholics. The Protestants were only one-tenth of the population, but owned nine-tenths of the landed property, held all high offices of state, constituted the aristocracy, abhorred the French and were devoted to the connection with England. The Dissenters comprised about one-fifth of the population and were mainly engaged in trade and manufacture in the province of Ulster. The Catholics numbered rather more than three million out of a total population of four and a half million. They were mainly peasants, living in misery and poverty on the estates of the Protestant landed gentry, but also included prosperous merchants and a small number of landed gentry.

Catholics and Dissenters had come together in the Society of United Irishmen, finding common cause in opposition to exploitation by England. The Catholic peasantry had organised themselves under the style of Defenders. The Catholic gentry and merchants had also come together in a General Committee.

The army in Ireland numbered about 30,000, 12,000 being troops of the line and the remainder militia. At least 16,000 of the militia were Catholics and a great number of them sworn Defenders.

Tone summarised this memorial by saying that it made clear that it was in the interest of France to separate Ireland from England. An attempt to do so was bound to succeed, for the reasons that the Dissenters and Catholics were organised and eager to shake off English tyranny, and that harmony and co-operation between them was certain; that the government could not rely on the army and that by proper measures the navy could be suborned; and finally, if affairs were as he had stated, the Protestant aristocracy would be completely unable to make a stand.

In his second memorial, Tone laid down that a body of French troops should be landed in Ireland, with a general of established reputation, who was known by name there. If possible, 20,000 men should be sent, 15,000 to land near Dublin, and the remaining 5,000 near Belfast. An expedition of that size could seize the entire country, without striking a blow, and the government would fall to pieces in a [74] matter of days. If the Directory could not spare so many, then 5,000 was the very smallest number to ensure success. The landing should be in the North, where probable supporters were best armed and organised. He thought that the militia would join with the invaders, if they saw a reasonable prospect of success. If only 5,000 men were sent, he still believed that the militia would come over, but could not positively assert that they would.

Immediately after the landing, a manifesto should be published, disavowing any thought of conquest by the French, proclaiming freedom of religion to all sects, declaring protection of persons and property, and inviting the people to join the republican standard, and to organise a national convention, for the purpose of framing a government.

Tone stated that, if only a thousand French landed, the peasantry would rise as one man to join them. A proclamation should be addressed to the Irishmen serving in the English navy, exhorting them to seize the vessels and sail them to Irish ports; reminding them of the hardships and injustices they suffered in the English service and offering them fair shares in rich prize money. This proclamation would undermine discipline in the navy, and combined with the setting-up of an independent Irish government, would render the navy vulnerable. The command of the seas by the English navy was essential to English policy of containing and then defeating Republican France. Clearly, any plan to weaken English sea power would have great attractions for the Directory.

On the part of the Irish people, the first step should be to raise as many soldiers as they had arms to put into their hands, which, Tone said, would be the only limitation on their numbers. A national convention should be called. The General Committee of the

Catholics, joined by delegates from the Dissenters, would represent nine-tenths of the population. The convention should issue a number of proclamations, declaring the independence of the country, calling the militia to the national standard and recalling all Irishmen from the dominions of Great Britain. An address should be made to the people of England and Scotland, warning them by the examples of America and France that it was impossible to conquer a whole people determined to be free, and pointing out the ruinous cost of attempting to subdue such a revolution. If this did not have the desired effect, the next step should be to confiscate all English property in Ireland and appropriate it to the national exchequer.

Perhaps Tone let his enthusiasm run away with him in representing that the peasantry would rise in great numbers, that the Defenders were organised throughout the country and that they and the Dissenters would join in instant support. He wildly over-estimated the proportion of Irishmen serving in the British navy and under-estimated the strength of the armed forces in Ireland. However, he emphasised throughout the vital importance of a large, well-equipped and imposing force, led by a general of high reputation, in attracting the desired response. And who knows what would have been the outcome of such a landing? Besides, Tone was prepared to risk his own life, whatever the size of the force despatched, and, no doubt, felt justified in using all possible arguments to induce the French to mount a formidable invasion. Moreover, they did not rely entirely on his version of the state of feeling in Ireland, as will be shown later.

The day after his talk with General Clarke, he called by request on Madgett, whom he found in high spirits, and who told him that everything was going as well as possible. They went together to Delacroix and Tone learnt, to his dismay, that it was proposed to send a

Capuchin friar, called Fitzsimons, to Ireland to establish liaison with Tone's friends there. Tone told Madgett that he was violently opposed to letting any priest
into the business at all. He wanted a military man,
whom he could trust, and Fitzsimons had been out of
Ireland for twenty or thirty years. Madgett, he
thought, was much more sanguine than he was. In
response to questioning, he told Madgett that he had
seen Carnot, and Madgett was put out at this, wanting
to keep all the strings in his own hands.

His next Journal entry reads, 'March 17, St Patrick's
Day. Dined *alone* in the Champs Elysées. Sad! Sad!'.

On 21 March, he went again to General Clarke, as
arranged. *'Damn it and rot it for me,* he has not yet
got my memorials.' They made an appointment for
five days later, and Tone left in a rage; precious days
were being wasted. He decided to write out his
memorials again himself and bring them to Clarke
personally.

Madgett sent for him to tell him that he was going
to visit Irish prisoners-of-war, with two objectives,
first, to find 'Mr William Browne', Tone's brother
Matthew, and send him to Ireland, with instructions
from Tone; and second, to induce as many as possible
of the Irish prisoners to embark on privateers and
descend on the Irish coast to prepare the Irish people.
Tone thought that this scheme was 'damned nonsense',
but he could not persuade Madgett to abandon it. His
own ideas were very different. 'The way to manage
them is this: If they intend to use the Irish prisoners,
let them be marched down under other pretences to
the port from whence the embarkation is to be made.
When everything else is ready, let them send in a large
quantity of wine and brandy, a fiddle and some French
filles, and then, when Pat's heart is a little soft with
love and wine, send in two or three proper persons in
regimentals, and with green cockades in their hats,

to speak to them, of whom I will very gladly be one. I think, in that case, it would not be very hard to per- suade him to take a trip once more to Ireland, just to see his *people* a little.' Madgett also asked him to draw up a manifesto which the French commander should publish on landing.

Tone's spirits were beginning to flag. 'It is inconceivable the solitude I live in here. Sometimes I am most dreadfully out of spirits, and it is no wonder. Losing the society of a family that I dote upon, and that loves me dearly, and living in Paris, amongst utter strangers, like an absolute *Chartreux*.' But he headed each chapter in his Journal, *Nil Desperandum*.

On 27 March, he had a long conversation with Clarke, who had read his two memorials and praised them highly. He told Clarke that he wished for a commission in the French army, so that he would not be hanged as a traitor if caught. Clarke replied that he was sure that could be arranged. Having arranged to call on Clarke once a week regularly, to see how affairs progressed, he took his leave, feeling more hopeful and better pleased with Clarke than he had been.

He had now spent six weeks in Paris. Because of the nature of his mission, he thought it wise to avoid striking up casual acquaintances. This solitary existence was hard on a man of his convivial temperament and he unburdened himself again in his Journal. 'I do not know a soul; I speak the language with great difficulty; I live in taverns, which I detest: I cannot be always reading.... I return to my apartment which is, notwithstanding, a very neat one, as if I was returning to gaol and finally I go to bed at night as if I was mounting the guillotine. I do lead a dog's life of it here, that is the truth of it; my sole resource is the opera.'

He went to see the Council of the Five Hundred, the French House of Commons. 'It is certainly the first assembly in Europe and the worst accommodated. They are likewise very disorderly ... but it is the same impetuosity that makes them redoubtable in the field and disorderly in the Senate. As to their appearance, it was extremely plain. But it is very little matter what they look like. They have humbled all Europe thus far, with their blue pantaloons and unpowdered locks.' They reminded him of his old masters the General Committee, except that the Committee looked more like gentlemen and were more orderly.

At further meetings with Clarke and Madgett, Tone learned with dismay that the idea was being pursued of landing bands of irregulars or Chouans, partly French convicts and partly prisoners-of-war, on the coasts of Ireland and England to harass and distract the authorities. He succeeded in killing the plan, pointing out that it would only alert the English army and militia, and cause the useless slaughter of Irish peasants who might join the irregulars, thus prejudicing the chances of a proper rising.

April 1796 started badly for Tone. He learned that John Keogh had been arrested and that several others had absconded to avoid imprisonment. Through Madgett, he met a physician called Aherne, who was to be sent to Ireland. Aherne suspected that Clarke was not honest. Tone was alarmed, remembering that Clarke had told him he was related to Lord Caher and the Butlers, and to Fitzgibbon by marriage, and remembering also Clarke's notion that the Irish aristocracy might join a movement for independence. As the month went on, he found that Clarke had become very secretive, and never had any news for him. But Delacroix told him that an expedition of 10,000 men would be ready by the end of May; the French army in Italy under Bonaparte had three great victories, and he moved from the Hotel des Etrangeres, 'where I have been fleeced like ten thousand devils' to Aherne's lodgings, which he hoped would be cheaper and more comfortable. He dined in [79] the Champs Elysées with Madgett and Aherne to celebrate the good news and afterwards walked around and saw the French soldiery dancing in groups under the trees with their wives and mistresses. 'Judge the humour I was in, with near two bottles of Burgundy in my head, whether I did not enjoy the spectacle. How often did I wish for my dearest love. Returned to the Restaurateur and indeed drank off another bottle, which made three.... Bed, slept like a top.'

He decided, since he could get nothing out of Clarke, to go directly to Carnot again, and presented himself at the Luxembourg on 2 May. Carnot told him that, before any final decision could be made, the Directory would have to send someone to Ireland, to ascertain whether the people were in fact friendly towards the French. 'This was a staggering blow to me, to find myself no farther advanced at the end of three months.' Then Clarke entered and clearly was not pleased to see Tone with Carnot. Tone felt all his hopes vanish. Delacroix was at odds with the Directory and might be dismissed at any moment. Madgett had no real authority, and did not trust Clarke. 'I began to think of my family and cottage again. I fancy it will be my lot at last to bury them and myself in the back woods of America.'

While waiting in this despondent state for any news from the Directory, he occupied himself in preparing further memorials and proclamations for Madgett and Clarke. Thinking again about the future, he took counsel with Madgett on the relative advantages of settling in America or France. His small capital of 400 *louis d'or* would go much further in France than in America. After several days anxious consideration he wrote to his wife, to Rowan and Dr Reynolds at the end of May, saying he had decided to settle in France, and asking his wife to convert all their property into

specie, to buy *louis d'or* at the Bank of Philadelphia, and to sail for France with their family on the first available vessel.

He admired the French. 'The men are agreeable and the women enchanting.... The English women have handsome faces, but for figure and fashion, they do not approach the French; and they (the French) walk so incomparably, and their language is so adapted to conversation, that they all appear to have wit.' Their morality was another matter. 'For "casual fruition", go to London, or indeed, rather to Paris, but if you wish to be happy, choose your companion at home.' France, and Paris in particular, reacting from the Terror, had plunged into a whirlwind of pleasure. Tone learnt that many deputies had availed themselves of their situation to secure the possession of beautiful women. The successes of the army, and the rise of a new rich class through war profiteering and currency inflation, gave impetus to extravagant living.... The theatres were packed every night and the people danced in the streets.

June passed wearily enough. Tone was now reduced to thirteen *louis d'or,* which would last him but another month. He informed Clarke of his precarious financial situation and the General promised that he would have a commission in the French army within the month. His Journal for 27 June reads, 'A sad rainy day, and I am not well, and the blue devils torment me.'

At this next meeting with Clarke, the General read from a document he had apparently received from an Irish source, giving an account of the situation in Ireland which confirmed everything Tone had written. Clarke would not divulge his source. Unknown to Tone, Lord Edward Fitzgerald and Arthur O'Connor, United Irishmen, had arrived in Hamburg and had forwarded a memorandum to Paris through the French representative. This may well have been the docu- ment Clarke had in his hands. Whatever its provenance, it firmly established Tone's credit with the Directory.

By July he had changed his opinion of General Clarke and blamed Aherne and Madgett for turning him against the General. 'He is a tall, handsome, proper young man, with a face like a cherubim.' Clarke was then thirty-one and went on to a brilliant career, being made Duc de Feltre, and holding high office under both Napoleon and Louis XVIII.

Bonaparte continued his successes in Italy, and the Pope and the King of Naples sent ambassadors to Paris to negotiate terms. Tone wrote, 'I am heartily glad that old Priest is at last laid under contribution in his turn. Many a long century he and his predecessors have been fleecing all Europe, but the day of retribution is come at last.' On 5 July he learned that the vessel carrying his letters to America had been taken by an English ship.

The next day, Clarke told him that General Hoche, who would command the Irish expedition, was coming shortly to Paris, and that, on his arrival, everything would be settled. On 12 July, he was summoned to the Luxembourg. 'The door opened and a very handsome, well made young fellow, in brown coat and nankeen pantaloons, entered.' It was Hoche, five years younger than Tone, and a rival to Bonaparte in reputation and achievement. He had a sabre cut down his forehead, eyebrow and one side of his nose, but it did not disfigure him. He had read Tone's memorials and they proceeded to discuss them. Clarke arrived, with an invitation to dine with Carnot. 'This was a grand day; I dined with the President of the Executive Directory of France, beyond all comparison the most illustrious station in Europe. I am very proud of it, because it has come fairly in the line of my duty, and I have made no unworthy sacrifices to obtain it. I like Carnot extremely, and Hoche, I think, yet more.'

Six days later, he was commissioned Chef de Brigade, or Colonel, in the French army, and was embraced by Clarke as a fellow officer. 'I am proud as Punch. Who would have thought this, the day I left the Lough of Belfast?' He drew a month's pay, which relieved his immediate necessities, although he later was obliged to draw on Philadelphia for £50, so that he could equip himself and have some money in his pocket. Later in July, he received a letter from Rowan, dated 30 March, and sent by private messenger. He was much relieved to find that his family were well, and that his brother Matthew had arrived in America in December. This was the first family news he had received since he left New York six months before. He immediately wrote to his wife and Rowan, repeating his previous instructions for the removal of his family and property to France, and entrusted the letters to the American Consul, who promised safe delivery. Hoche departed for his headquarters in Rennes early in August. Tone was to follow with General Cherin, Chief of Staff, in about a fortnight, but as it turned out, did not leave Paris until 17 September. Now that the expedition was being organised he chafed at this delay. He went to the opera nearly every night, and called on Madgett, Clarke and Cherin, but time still hung very heavy on his hands. He bethought himself to write a sketch of his life to the time he landed in France. He wrote from memory, admitting that he might be inaccurate in the dates. For the period from July 1792 to April 1795, he referred the reader to his diaries, but these were either incomplete or were lost in America. Save for short periods in 1792 and early 1793, we have no first-hand account from him of the events of that period.

On 14 August he put on his regimentals for the first time. 'Pleased as a little boy in his first breeches. Foolish enough, but not unpleasant. Walked about Paris to show myself: Huzza! Citoyen Wolfe Tone, Chef de Brigade in the service of the Republic.'

At length, on 17 September, he received orders to depart and set out for Rennes. But again he was tormented by delays. The army there was prepared but the navy lagged behind and Hoche posted to Brest to hurry them. Finding a shortage of seamen, he gave orders to press men all along the coast, as far as Bordeaux. It was going to be a winter campaign, and Tone wrote in his Journal, 'No matter, we are better able to stand it than those who will be opposed to us. The country gentlemen of Ireland, with their warm feather beds, their beef and claret, will make, I think, no great figure before our grenadiers, who have been seasoned these four years to all manner of hardships and privations.'

On 16 October, Hoche narrowly escaped assassination in the streets of Rennes; papers found in the lodgings of the assassin made Tone suspect that he was an English agent. Tone struck up a close friendship with Colonel Shee, an uncle of Clarke, who had been a cavalry officer for thirty-six years and who kept him informed on the progress of the preparations. By Hoche's express orders, Tone was known as Mr Smith, an American, and after the first day at Rennes, Hoche treated him with reserve, to preserve his incognito. Before they departed for Brest to embark, Hoche appointed Tone to the rank of Adjutant-General. Tone's liking for Hoche was reciprocated. In a chance private moment, Hoche said to him, 'I am not a man to make professions, but I beg you will, on all occasions, look upon me as your friend, and treat me accordingly.'

The journey to Brest took eight days. Tone exclaims 'I like this life of all things. There is a gaiety, and a carelessness about military men, which interests me infinitely'. But on the way, he was shown a copy of the English *Morning Post* of 24 September, which contained bad news for him. Russell and Neilson had been arrested for high treason. He could only hope that the expedition would reach Ireland in time to save his friends. On arrival in Brest on 1 November, Tone set to work on an address to the Irish people, to be printed in Brest and distributed on landing. On Hoche's orders, an officer named MacSheehy was sent to Ireland on an American vessel, to bring back information, up to date, on the state of the country. Tone told MacSheehy he should call on Oliver Bond and Richard McCormick, and what he should say to them. Again by Hoche's orders, Tone recruited fifty Irishmen from among prisoners-of-war at Pontazen, near Brest. He observed with misgiving that the French admiral, Villaret de Joyeuse, was lukewarm about the undertaking, and that relations between the army and the navy were bad; a staff officer wounded a naval lieutenant in a duel. The Spanish fleet and dockyards had been placed at the disposal of the French Directory by the Treaty of San Ildefonso in August 1796. He raged to Colonel Shee about the Spaniards remaining in Toulon; they should be in Brest, and with the invasion fleet would chase away the English navy. Without them, the invasion fleet would be no match for the English.

What seemed better news came early in November; Hoche succeeded in having Joyeuse replaced. The new naval commander-in-chief was Morard de Galles. Hoche would have preferred Latouche Treville, who had shown real leadership, but he was not available. Morard de Galles was not the happiest choice. As a diversionary tactic, Hoche assigned 1,050 men of the

Legion Noire, the scum of the army, to an American officer, Colonel Tate, with orders to attack Bristol [85] and burn it to the ground. Tone translated Tate's instructions, to reduce to ashes the third city of Britain, which would involve great human misery. But the British, he thought, had done worse in America and Ireland. 'I do not think my morality of feeling is much improved by my promotion to the rank of Adjutant-General. The truth is, I hate the very name of England; I hated her before my exile; I hate her since, and I will hate her always.'

Hoche gave him 'a mortal fright' by stealing off to spend two days and nights with 'a charming little aristocrat'. All her relations were Chouans, that is, royalist brigands, who might well have waylaid and killed him. 'I was very angry with him, which, as I never did a foolish thing myself in my life for the sake of a woman, was but reasonable.'

The great day, for which Tone had worked so hard and so long, came at last. On 2 December he received his orders to embark on the *Indomptable*, a ship of the line of eighty guns. The invasion was on.

6
Bantry Bay

Before embarking, Tone wrote a long letter to his
wife. He assumed that she had received his letter of
July, and was by now on the high seas en route to
Le Havre, and exposed to the dangers of a winter passage. 'I trust in God you will get safe and well, and
that, by the time you will receive this, we shall have
finished our business, in which case, you and I will
devote the remainder of our lives to each other, for
I am truly weary of the perpetual separation that we
have lived in, I may almost say, from the day of our
marriage.'

He told her of the expedition about to sail, and of
his high hopes of success, if they arrived safely in Ireland. If intercepted by the British fleet, they would
fight to the last extremity. 'I would not write thus to
terrify you needlessly, but long before you receive
my letter, the affair will be over, one way or the other:
I hope happily for us, in which case I once more
promise you never to quit you again for any tempta-
tion of fame, honour or interest. After all we have
suffered, a little tranquillity is now surely due to us.'
He went on to advise her as to what she should do in
various eventualities. If he was killed but the expedition succeeded, she should go at once to Ireland, and
he was confident that his friends would see to her
future and that of his family. In case of his death and
the failure of the invasion, she should apply to Carnot,
General Clarke, Colonel Shee, and General Hoche. If

the French authorities were unable or unwilling to help her, he hoped that his brother Matt would stay with her, 'as a faithful friend to you, and a father to my darling babies'.

He then turned to the bright side. 'Remember, I am now in the high road to fortune, and, I hope, to fame, for, if we succeed, I think I may say I have earned some reputation, but, I can also say, that neither fame nor fortune are an object with me, further than as they will enable me to manifest my sense of your goodness and virtues.' He hoped to obtain commissions for his brothers Matthew and Arthur, and to retain, at least, his own rank as Adjutant-General.

He mentioned a third possibility, that the expedition should be beaten back, but that he should return safely. 'In that case, I think I shall be able to retain my pay, as Adjutant-General, which, as things go here, will be a vast addition to our little fortune; I will then buy or hire a small farm, within a few miles of Paris, and devote the remander of my life to making you happy and educating our children.'

His letter ends 'I write in a state of the utmost anxiety and incertitude... uncertain of your fate and that of our children, uncertain of my own, in which you and they are so deeply interested, I think it is hardly possible to conceive a more painful and anxious situation; add to this, that I am obliged to devour my uneasiness, from the fear of appearing disheartened at the moment of embarkation.... If we fail, at least, it is in an honourable cause, and on just principles.... God Almighty forever bless and preserve you. Adieu, my dearest life and soul. Kiss my darling babies for me ten thousand times, and love me ever as I love you.

'Once more adieu!'

Tone embarked on board the *Indomptable,* a ship of the line, on 2 December, but the fleet did not sail until the 15th. In all, there were forty-five vessels and

a total military force of 14,750 men, truly a formidable armada. There were eighteen ships of the line,
thirteen frigates, six corvettes, brigs, and luggers, and
eight transports, including an ammunition ship. The
ships of the line were so called because they were
large enough and carried enough guns to lie in the line
of battle. With the exception of the *Indomptable* of
eighty guns and a smaller ship of forty-four guns, the
ships in the fleet carried seventy-four guns. The frigates
carried from thirty to forty guns, had superior sailing
qualities and were used as look-outs and for trans-
mitting signals. The smaller corvettes and luggers were
fast and weatherly and could carry messages from
ship to ship.

Warships in those days carried what now seem
to have been very large crews. A ship of the line
needed at least five hundred men to work the vessel
with its huge spread of sail and to man the guns.
Each ship of the line in the French fleet also carried
between five hundred and six hundred soldiers, and
the frigates about half that number, with stores,
artillery and ammunition. Both ships and frigates
were square-rigged and, of course, completely dependent on the wind for motive power. They could not
sail nearer the wind than six points or 67½ degrees.
This meant that in order to reach an objective from
which the wind blew directly, they had to proceed by
broad zig-zags or tacks. With an unhandy crew ham-
pered by hundreds of soldiers around the decks, the
vessels could make only very slow progress when
tacking, as Tone found to his chagrin when they were
off Bantry Bay.

The commander-in-chief, Hoche, and the naval
commander, Admiral Morard de Galles, sailed in the
frigate *Fraternité* which also carried the money, the
plans and the proclamations for the expedition. The
second-in-command, General Grouchy, now remem-

bered for his inglorious part at Waterloo, sailed in another frigate, *L'Immortalité* with de Galles' deputy, Admiral Bouvet. With Tone in *L'Indomptable* were the staff officers, headed by General Cherin. Thus the command and the staff were divided between three vessels.

The French coast was dangerous to navigation, abounding in reefs and shoals. The British Admiralty, through its many spies in Brest, was well aware that an expedition was being organised, but was in doubt as to its destination. The Directory had put it about that Portugal was the target, and Hoche even had proclamations printed in Portuguese. A squadron of ships of the line cf the English Channel fleet, under Admiral Colpoys, was cruising west of Ushant, and an inshore squadron of frigates under the dashing Captain Pellew kept watch on the movements of the French fleet. The main English reserve of fifteen ships of the line was stationed at Spithead, off the Isle of Wight, 210 miles north-east of Ushant. The Irish coast was defended only by a sixty-four gun ship and six frigates stationed at Cork harbour.

The evening before they sailed, General Watrin paid a visit to Tone's ship, with the band of his regiment. Tone describes the scene. 'I went down into the great cabin, where all the officers mess, and where the music was playing. The cabin was ceiled with the firelocks intended for the expedition, the candlesticks were bayonets, stuck in the table, the officers were in their jackets and bonnets de police; some playing cards, others singing to the music; others conversing, and all in the highest spirits — once again I was delighted with the scene. At length Watrin and his band went off, and, as it was a beautiful moonlight night, the effect of the music on the water, diminishing as they receded from our vessel, was delicious.'

The harbour of Brest could be left by any one of

three channels. Admiral Morard de Galles rejected the northernmost, the Canal de Four, as it would have signalled to the British that their destination was Ireland. The main exit, the Iroise channel, twenty miles wide with ample depth of water, was open to the West, and was clearly the easiest to navigate, but Pellew's frigates were waiting outside. The third channel, the Raz de Sein, barely three miles wide with dangerous currents, had not been used before by a fleet. Despite the hazards of taking a large fleet with inexperienced crews through this passage, the admiral decided it was worth the risk, to mislead the British. Once safely out to sea, they could alter course unseen by the enemy.

On the morning of 15 December, with a fair wind from the east, the great ships weighed anchor, and sailed out the narrow passage from the inner harbour. Manoeuvring at such close quarters was beyond the competence of some of the captains, and after a series of collisions, the fleet had made only three leagues, and the admiral decided to anchor in Camaret Bay for the night.

The final departure was made the following day, 16 December in the early afternoon. The admiral had sent frigates the previous day to find out what the English were doing. The information they brought back convinced him, wrongly as it turned out, that the enemy did not know that the French were on their way out to sea. To countermand his previous orders, de Galles made a signal that the fleet should leave by the main, and safe, Iroise channel. Darkness was falling, the fleet was scattered ahead of the admiral's frigate and the signal was either not received or not understood. The scene soon became one of wild confusion. Rockets were fired from the admiral's vessel to show his position, and the corvette *Atalante* dashed into the middle of the fleet firing guns to attract attention to the change of course. With great daring,

Pellew brought his frigate close to the French and to confuse them further, sent up rockets and fired guns.

The *Seduisant,* a ship of the line with 1,300 on board struck rocks in the treacherous Raz de Sein and all except forty-five perished. Seventeen vessels, including the frigate *L'Immortalité* with Bouvet and Grouchy on board and Tone's ship *L'Indomptable* succeeded in gaining the open sea through the Raz. A further seventeen made for the Iroise channel. The two groups were thirty miles apart and it was blowing hard. It was by a fortunate chance that they met two days later, when it fell a flat calm.

But there was no sign of the *Fraternité,* with the two commanders-in-chief on board. She was one of the last to leave her anchorage in Camaret Bay. She steered west through the Iroise in the dark December night, followed by one ship of the line. Next morning two frigates joined them, one bringing the erroneous news that the whole fleet had passed through the Raz and was ahead to the west. In fact, one group was astern and the other to the south. On 18 December Bouvet's group was only about twenty miles from de Galles, and on a clear day could have been sighted by the mast-head look-out. But there was a thick fog, and the extraordinary fact is that the *Fraternité* arrived back at La Rochelle on 14 January 1797, without ever again seeing the main fleet. On 18 December, then, the situation was that a fleet of thirty-four vessels was on course for its destination, but plans, money, proclamations and commanders-in-chief were missing, four vessels were separated from the main fleet, several stragglers unaccounted for, and one vessel sunk. It was not the most promising beginning, but the elements of a successful expedition were still there.

Their destination, Bantry Bay, was kept secret until the fleet had sailed. Tone does not mention it until

19 December. He had all along been in favour of a
landing in the north, where organised support could
be expected, or near Dublin, so that the seat of government could be taken. The advantages of Bantry Bay
had been pointed out to the Directory in a memorial
from United Irishman E. J. Lewins in November 1796.
It was undefended, easy of access and the people
were Defenders and enemies of England. Cork,
undefended, was only two days away and its capture
would make the French masters of the south. The
French admirals saw that it was the nearest point on
the Irish coast to Brest, thirty-six hours sailing with a
favourable wind. Bruix, naval chief-of-staff to the
expedition, prepared excellent detailed instructions
as to the passage to Ireland, anchoring in the Bay and
landing the troops. The Bay itself was a magnificent
stretch of water, eighteen miles long and three to four
miles wide, with deep water right to the head.

The captains had been given sealed packets with
instructions in case of separation. These were now
opened and they learned that they should make for
Mizen Head, and cruise off there for five days. If by
then the rest of the fleet had not arrived, or if they
had not got fresh instructions they were to sail to the
mouth of the Shannon, and cruise there for three
days. If still no instructions came, they were to return
to Brest. On 21 December, the fleet was in sight of
the Irish coast off Bantry Bay. Tone noted in his
Journal:

> Is that such a separation of our forces (only seven
> or eight absent), as, under all the circumstances,
> will warrant our following the letter of our orders,
> to the certain failure of the expedition? If Grouchy
> and Bouvet be men of spirit and decision, they will
> land immediately, and trust to their success for justi-
> fication. If they be not, and if this day passes with-

out our seeing the General [Hoche], I much fear the game is up. I am in undescribable anxiety, and [93] Cherin, who commands aboard, is a poor creature, to whom it is vain to speak; not but I believe he is brave enough, but he has a little mind. There cannot be imagined a situation more provokingly tantalising than mine at this moment, within view, almost within reach, of my native land, and uncertain whether I shall ever set my foot on it. We are now, nine o'clock, at the rendezvous appointed; stood in for the coast till twelve, when we were near enough to toss a biscuit ashore; at twelve tacked and stood out again, so now we have begun our cruise of five days in all its forms, and shall, in obedience to the letter of our instructions, ruin the expedition, and destroy the remnant of the French navy, with a precision and punctuality which will be truly edifying. We opened Bantry Bay, and, in all my life, rage never entered so deeply into my heart as when we turned our backs on the coast.

That morning a number of Irish pilots came alongside, and were taken on board to guide the French to their anchorage. The east wind continued; it had been favourable for the passage from Brest, but was almost dead ahead in entering Bantry Bay, that is, as adverse as possible. Faulty navigation had brought them too far west towards Dursey Head, adding to the difficulty of getting into the bay. By 22 December, only half the fleet had entered. Tone wrote, 'these delays are dreadful to my impatience.... According to appearances, Bouvet and Grouchy are resolved to proceed; that is a great point gained, however. Two o'clock, we have been tacking ever since eight this morning, and I am sure we have not gained one hundred yards; the wind is right ahead, and the fleet dispersed, several being far to leeward.'

Tone did not appreciate the enormous difficulties [94] facing the French captains, manoeuvring great clumsy ships to windward in narrow waters, with inexperienced crews and constant danger of collision with other vessels of the fleet. A bitterly cold east wind blowing off the snow-clad mountains, and decks crowded with sea-sick soldiers, made matters no easier. Bouvet then made a bad mistake by anchoring in mid-channel, ignoring Bruix's instructions to anchor inside Bere Island, where there was excellent shelter, no matter what quarter the wind blew from. He may have thought, and perhaps rightly, that this manoeuvre called for seamanship his crews did not possess. On the night of the 23rd a heavy gale from the east blew almost twenty of the fleet out to sea. Tone was in dread that the English would come upon them, and to salvage some honour from the situation, asked Cherin to give him the Legion des Francs, some 1,600 men, and artillery, and as many officers as would join him, and land them in Sligo Bay. This stirred Cherin to action, and with Tone and Colonel Waudre of the artillery, he boarded the frigate *L'Immortalité* for a council of war with Grouchy and Bouvet. The general agreed to go ahead with a landing, with the forces available, amounting to 6,400 men with four guns, as the ships blown outside had not returned. Tone recorded in his Journal:

> It is altogether an enterprise truly unique; we have not one guinea; we have not a tent; we have not a horse to draw our four pieces of artillery; the General in chief marches on foot; we leave all our baggage behind us; we have nothing but the arms in our hands, the clothes on our backs, and a good courage, but that is sufficient ... we are all as gay as larks. I never saw the French character better exemplified, than in this morning's business. Huzza!

I apprehend we are tonight 6,000 of the most careless fellows in Europe, for everybody is in the [95] most extravagant spirits on the eve of an enterprise which, considering our means, would make many people serious. I never liked the French half so well as tonight, and I can scarcely persuade myself that the loungers of the Boulevards, and the soldiers I see about me, are of the same hemisphere. To judge the French rightly, or at least to see the bright part of their characters, you must see them, not in Paris, but in the camp. It is in the armies that the Republic exists. My enemy, the wind, seems just now, at eight o'clock, to relent a little, so we may reach Bantry by tomorrow.

The enemy has now had four days to recover from his panic, and prepare to receive us; so much the worse, but I do not mind it. We purpose to make a race for Cork, as if the devil were in our bodies, and when we are fairly there, we will stop for a day or two to take breath, and look about us.

But the 24th passed with virtually nothing accomplished, for the vessels made no worthwhile progress towards a landing place and Grouchy made no effort to get troops ashore. Christmas Day saw Tone devoured by the most gloomy reflections. The wind got up and boatwork, which was possible for resolute men on the 24th, became out of the question. In desperation, Tone proposed that they should sail to the Shannon, land there and march on Limerick, which he thought would be easily taken, and then press on to the north. Cherin and the other officers agreed to this plan, but it was impossible to communicate with Grouchy and Admiral Bouvet, as they were two leagues ahead in the *Immortalité,* and the sea was so rough that no boat could live in it. Tone saw clearly now the errors that had been made. 'I cannot conceive for what reason the two commanders-in-chief are shut up together in a frigate. Surely they should be on board the flagship [*L'Indomptable*]. But that is not the first misfortune resulting from this arrangement. Had General Hoche remained, as he ought, on board the *Indomptable*, with his État Major [staff], he would not have been separated and taken by the English, as he most probably is.... Our first capital error was in setting sail too late from the bay of Camaret, by which means we were obliged to pass the Raz in the night, which caused the loss of the *Seduisant*, the separation of the fleet, the capture of the General, and above all, the loss of time resulting from all this, and which is never to be recovered. Our second error was in losing an entire day in cruising off the bay, when we might have entered and effected a landing with thirty-five sail, which would have secured everything, and now our third error is having our Commander-in-Chief separated from the État Major, which renders all communication utterly impossible. My prospects at this hour are as gloomy as possible. I see nothing before me, unless a miracle be wrought in our favour, but the ruin of the expedition, the slavery of my country, and my own destruction. Well, if I am to fall, at least I will sell my life as dear as individual resistance can make it. So now I have made up my mind. I have a merry Christmas of it today.'

The gale increased in violence on Christmas Day, and at 6 p.m. the admiral's frigate, *L'Immortalité*, began to drag her anchors, and was being driven by terrific squalls towards Bere Island, less than a mile away. The Admiral cut his cable and made for the open sea, despite the protests of Grouchy, whom he had not consulted. The Irish pilots had forecast a violent gale with the wind veering south, and Admiral Bouvet feared that his ships would be trapped in the bay and probably wrecked. He signalled by megaphone and gun fire to the other vessels to follow his example, but in the pitch dark and howling wind his orders were not understood. At half-past six, Bedout, captain of Tone's ship, was astonished to see a frigate loom up on their quarter with shouts of 'Coupez vos cables, appareillez!' and scud past them. This was a frigate dispatched by Admiral Bouvet, but Bedout suspected that she might be an English frigate which had been lurking at the head of the bay, fifteen miles eastward, which was trying to confuse the French with these orders to cut their cables and get under way. He decided to wait until the morning. Tone's Journal continues:

The morning is now come, the gale continues, and the fog is so thick that we cannot see a ship's length ahead; so here we lie in the utmost uncertainty and anxiety.... Certainly we have been persecuted by a strange fatality, from the very night of our departure, to this hour. We have lost two commanders-in-chief; of four admirals not one remains; we have lost one ship of the line, that we know of, and probably many others of which we know nothing; we have been now six days in Bantry Bay, within five hundred yards of the shore, without being able to effectuate a landing; we have been dispersed four times in four days, and, at this moment, of forty-three sail, of which the expedition consisted, we can muster of all sizes but fourteen. There only wants our falling in with the English, to complete our destruction... all our hopes are now reduced to get back in safety to Brest.... The enemy has had seven days to prepare for us, and three, or perhaps four days more before we could arrive at Cork; and we are now too much reduced, in all respects, to make the attempt with any prospect of success — so, all is over! ... Well, England has not had such an escape since the Spanish Armada, and that expedition, like ours, was defeated by the weather; the elements fight against us, and courage is here of no avail. Well, let me think no more about it; it is lost, and let it go! I am now a Frenchman, and must regulate my future plans accordingly. I hope the Directory will not dismiss me the service for this unhappy failure, in which, certainly, I have nothing personally to reproach myself with; and in that case, I shall be rich enough to live as a peasant. If God Almighty sends me my dearest love and darling babies in safety, I will buy or rent a little spot, and have done with the world forever. I shall neither be great, nor famous, nor powerful, but I may be happy. God knows whether I shall ever reach France myself, and, in that case, what will become of my family! It is horrible to me to think of. Oh, my life and soul, my darling babies, shall I ever see you again?

On 26 December, several vessels dragged their anchors, and were given permission to make for the open sea. On the 27th, a council of war was held by the remaining officers. Considering the reduced size of the fleet and the probability that the English were now well aware of their presence in Bantry Bay, and had time to muster their forces, it was agreed that they should make for the mouth of the Shannon and cruise there for five days in the hope that more of the scattered fleet would join them. But when they got outside the bay later that day, it came on to blow a hurricane. Tone's ship, the *Indomptable*, running under bare poles, was pooped by a heavy sea which came over her stern, and stove in the quarter gallery and one of the dead-lights in the great cabin, which filled with water to a depth of three feet. Tone had just fallen asleep in his hammock. Awakened by the shock, he thought his last hour had come. 'Hear- ing the water rolling in the cabin beneath me, and two or three of the officers mounting in their shirts, as wet as if they had risen from the bottom of the sea, I concluded instantly that the ship had struck and was filling with water and that she would sink directly; but I was soon relieved by the appearance of one of the officers who explained to us the accident.'

On 29 December they reached their rendezvous at the mouth of the Shannon, but now there were only five vessels in company with the *Indomptable*. Yielding to the inevitable, Bedout made the signal to steer for France. They arrived back at Brest on 1 January 1797. Tone observed, 'I am utterly astonished that we did not see a single English ship of war, going nor coming back.'

What had happened to the *Immortalité*, with Grouchy and Bouvet on board? After gaining the open sea on Christmas Day about 7 p.m., she was driven westward for three days by furious gales and battered by tremendous seas. On 29 December, the gales abated and were succeeded by a moderate breeze from the west. It seemed to Grouchy that this favourable wind gave them a chance to enter Bantry Bay again and he pressed Bouvet to make the attempt. The admiral weighed up the situation. He thought that there was little hope that the scattered fleet would join together in the bay. He had only one anchor and no sound cable. He feared that the English squadrons under Admirals Colpoys and Bridport would appear at any moment and the French would be no match for them. Besides, the element of surprise had been lost; the enemy had ample warning and time to assemble their land forces. It seemed to him that there was only one course open to him, to return to France, and make a fresh start, with the fleet re-provisioned and united under their commander-in-chief. Despite Grouchy's angry protests, he set course for Brest and arrived there on 1 January, two hours before Tone's ship.

The misadventures of the frigate *Fraternité*, carrying the two commanders-in-chief, General Hoche and Admiral Morard de Galles, complete the melancholy story of the expedition, and add an element of mystery, tinged with a suggestion of perfidy. Accompanied by a ship of the line and two other frigates, the *Fraternité* was out in the Atlantic, sixty miles to the south of the Irish coast, on 21 December, when the main fleet was taking on local Irish pilots to guide them into Bantry Bay. The following night, the *Fraternité* sighted lights away to the north-east. The French fleet had strict orders to darken ship at night, and de Galles took these lights to be those of an English squadron and steered west-north-west to avoid them. They were, in fact, the lights of his own ships. This manoeuvre carried him further away from the Irish coast, and during the night the other ships separated from him and were nowhere to be seen at morning. The strong easterly wind which was so frustrating to the main fleet in trying to enter Bantry Bay, was equally adverse to the *Fraternité*. The wind rose to gale force, and on Christmas Day the frigate was running before it under bare poles. The following morning they sighted a vessel to the north-east. She made no response to their signals and they took her to be an enemy. Crowding on sail, the *Fraternité* ran before the storm in imminent danger of driving herself under in the tremendous seas. Some of the guns were thrown overboard to lighten her. She was carrying nearly 300 soldiers in addition to her crew of 200. After thirty-six hours of this terrifying headlong career, plunging and rolling, they had shaken off the unknown vessel and were then about 200 miles to the south-west of the Irish coast. By 28 December the storm had blown itself out, the wind had changed to westerly and the frigate was able to steer again towards Bantry Bay. The tracks of the *Fraternité* and the *Immortalité* crossed each other, and they must have been quite close, the commanders-in-chief making for the planned landing place and their seconds-in-command heading for France after abandoning the invasion attempt. Two French ships and a frigate were sighted, signals were exchanged and a despatch was delivered to de Galles with the news of the loss of the *Seduisant,* and of the hazardous situation of the remaining ships in Bantry Bay. Despite the gloomy outlook, the Admiral decided to continue for the bay, and by noon on 30 December his frigate was twenty-eight miles south-west of Dursey Island. Inexplicably, though the wind was favourable, de Galles failed to make his landfall. The records show that he stood out to sea again, as if afraid of going too close to a lee shore. Hoche and the admiral had a consultation on the afternoon of the 31st. By that time, there were no ships left in Bantry Bay, provisions were running dangerously low, one of the accompanying ships had sunk and another was barely seaworthy. Reluctantly, they abandoned hope and changed course for France, reaching Rochefort on 14 January 1797.

On 28 December, not a single French vessel remained in Bantry Bay. To add yet another freakish turn to the confused pattern of events, a number of the fleet which had been kept out in the Atlantic by storms now straggled in, and some reached the head of the bay and anchored off Whiddy Island. By 1 January there were eight ships of the line, four frigates and a transport at anchor in the bay, with 4,000 trooops in all aboard. Ironically, had Hoche and de Galles held on their course for the bay on 31 December, they would have found this remnant of the fleet waiting them. What would Hoche have done?

The shore defences were pitifully inadequate and [102] ill prepared to resist a landing. There were only 400 infantry and a troop or two of cavalry at Bantry. But the local people deceived the French into believing that a far stronger force was ready to receive them, talking of thousands of troops and a squadron of six ships of the line at Cork. The French officers held a council of war. They had no plans, were short of provisions and were afraid of being trapped in the bay. They decided to cruise outside for a few days, and if no reinforcements arrived, to return to France. They were back in Brest on 14 January 1797.

Tone had been astonished by the absence of any English ships of war. The English admirals had Portugal uppermost in their minds as the destination of the French fleet, and when the weather deteriorated they thought that the French ships must surely have been scattered and could not reach Portugal against the adverse winds. Admiral Colpoys kept his squadron on station off Ushant, hoping to intercept stray French ships. Admiral Bridport was ordered by the Admiralty on 22 December to take his squadron to sea, but did not succeed in leaving Spithead until 4 January. Whatever criticism may be made of the incompetence of the French navy, the British were no better in those critical weeks.

The first news of the arrival of the French at Bantry Bay was sent to General Dalrymple in Cork by Richard White, landlord, on 22 December. He also organised the local yeomanry to oppose a landing, or, at least to make a show of resistance, and posted outposts on the mountains. He duly received his reward for these services, being raised to the peerage as Lord Bantry. The news did not reach the Admiralty in London until 31 December, nine days after the French had anchored off Bere Island.

Tone had confidently told the Directory that the

Veritas Company Limited
20 Shipquay Street
BT48
Tel. (028) 7126 6888
VAT No GB762678

Description	Qty	Cost
781856077057		
rom Cork To China	1	10.99
781586175994		
dith Stein and	1	12.75

otal To Pay:	23.74
ayment: Cash	30.00
hange Given:	6.26

PLEASE KEEP YOUR RECEIPT
www.veritas.ie

eceipt No:105308:20/04/11:1508:0003:01

VERITAS
BOOKS · GIFTS · ART
www.veritas.ie

VERITAS
BOOKS · GIFTS · ART
www.veritas.ie

VERITAS
BOOKS · GIFTS · ART
www.veritas.ie

VERITAS
BOOKS · GIFTS · ART
www.veritas.ie

VERITAS
BOOKS · GIFTS · ART
www.veritas.ie

VERITAS
BOOKS · GIFTS · ART
www.veritas.ie

VERITAS
BOOKS · GIFTS · ART
www.veritas.ie

VERITAS
BOOKS · GIFTS · ART
www.veritas.ie

VERITAS
BOOKS · GIFTS · ART
www.veritas.ie

VERITAS
BOOKS · GIFTS · ART
www.veritas.ie

VERITAS
BOOKS · GIFTS · ART
www.veritas.ie

VERITAS
BOOKS · GIFTS · ART

people would flock to the French colours if a landing was made in sufficient force. But the leaders, Keogh, Neilson, Russell and Teeling, were in prison and Lord Edward Fitzgerald and Arthur O'Connor were far away. Worse still, no one in Ireland, it seems, knew that the landing was to take place in Bantry Bay. Fear of interception by the English fleet was uppermost in the minds of the French, and their destination was kept secret until the ships were at sea. The Irish in Munster were not organised and there was no one to lead them. Nevertheless, had 14,000 seasoned French troops landed with artillery, arms and ammunition, the defence would have been brushed aside and Cork could have been taken. But the landing did not take place, and the cautious local people showed a loyalty to the government that was most heartening to General Dalrymple. It is fair conjecture that this loyalty was a delicate growth and that a successful landing would have evoked a different response. After all, the Irish rallied in their thousands to Humbert, when he landed at Killala, Co. Mayo in August 1798 with a force much inferior to that led by Hoche. To the Catholic hierarchy, of course, French revolutionary principles were anathema and rumours of a French invasion were met by pastorals exhorting the faithful to remain loyal to the government.

The expedition failed for a number of reasons. The worst disaster was the absence of the commander-in-chief, Hoche, from Bantry Bay on the fateful days from 21 to 24 December, when a landing could have been made. General Hoche was a daring and forceful commander and would not have let difficulties deter him. He probably chose to sail in a frigate rather than a ship of the line, because a frigate would have a far better chance of eluding capture by the English than the slower and more cumbersome flagship.

It remains to add a sinister footnote, by quoting

from Thomas Crofton Croker, an Irishman who was [104] an official in the British Admiralty from 1818 to 1850.

> And what is the true history of the failure of this expedition? The Editor has been told from the most unquestionable authority, that it was public confidence in the English funds — the trust of England in her Chancellor of the Exchequer. This is not the time or place to enter into more minute statements — but there can be no doubt whatever that the captain of the *Fraternité* had accepted a bribe of a considerable amount, to give the military and naval commanders-in-chief a cruise for a few weeks on the banks of Newfoundland, before landing them in Ireland; and that he performed this delicate act of secret service so well, that he boldly drew upon the English Government for double the amount agreed upon, which, however, was ultimately arranged to the perfect satisfaction of all parties concerned.[19]

Admiral de Galles was an experienced seaman, but he was fifty-five and in poor health. He had asked to be relieved of his command, pleading, in particular, his eyesight, which, he said, only permitted him with difficulty to distinguish objects at four paces. An unscrupulous captain could have had his way in recognising 'enemy' ships, altering course and keeping away from a landfall, with his commander so physically handicapped. The astonishment and exasperation felt by Tone are very evident from his Journal for 22 December: 'No news of the *Fraternité*; I believe it is the first instance of an Admiral in a clean frigate with moderate weather and moonlight nights, parting company with his fleet.' Is it possible that the captain of the frigate who misled Admiral de Galles as to the whereabouts of the fleet immediately after they had left Brest, was also in the pay of the English? Brest was swarming with English agents at the time.

December was a bad month to choose to sail out into the Atlantic; the delay was due to the disorganised state of the French navy, and for the same reason, the ships were ill-found and had insufficient provisions.

But despite all these mistakes and hazards, success was within their grasp, but, fatally, Grouchy showed no great urge to land his troops in the absence of Hoche. This hesitation was of a piece with his conduct at Waterloo. Defending himself after that catastrophe, Grouchy said, 'Inspiration in war is appropriate only to the commander-in-chief, and his lieutenants must confine themselves to executing orders.' Then, he showed no initiative, authority or energy; he took refuge in a literal obedience to orders.[20]

Tone saw the matter differently. 'They [the Staff] stared at me this morning [22 December], when I said that Grouchy was the man in the whole army who had the least reason to regret the absence of the General, and began to talk of responsibilities and difficulties, as if any great enterprise was without responsibility and difficulties.' It was only after Tone's near frenzied demands for some action that Grouchy agreed to go ahead, but even then, that last opportunity for a landing on 24 December was let slip, and the fate of the expedition was sealed.

The French naval historian, Captain Desbrière, put it very bluntly. 'From 20 December to 6 January, French ships were at anchor in Bantry Bay for seventeen consecutive days, with the single exception of the 28th, without the slightest obstacle from the English cruisers. No important mobilisation of troops had taken place, and the French would have been able to land six thousand men on 24 December, four thousand more on the 27th and four thousand others from 3 to 6 January.'[21]

Then there was the weather. The winds usually pre-
vailing at that time of year were south-westerly, and
would have enabled the French not only to reach
Bantry Bay but to sail right up to Whiddy Island. But
in Tone's words, 'The wind has hung in the East these
five weeks.' Not only was it adverse but it increased
to gale force. No wonder the Cork grandee, Lord
Shannon, hummed to himself with satisfaction:

> Ho, by my soul, 'tis a Protestant wind,
> Lillibulero, bullen-a-la.[22]

Tone was right. England had not had such an escape
since the Spanish Armada. As W. B. Yeats wrote
many years later, 'John Bull and the sea are friends.'[23]

Admiral Bouvet was made the scapegoat for the
failure of the expedition. The Directory deprived him
of his command and of his rank.

7
An Officer in the French Army

For a whole month after his landing back at Brest, Tone had not the heart to make a single entry in his Journal, which begins again on 31 January 1797. General Grouchy sent him to Paris with his dispatches and asked him to convey to the Directory his, Tone's, opinion of Grouchy's conduct during the expedition. Strangely enough after his outbursts against Grouchy in his Journal, Tone defended him, and took every opportunity to praise Grouchy's zeal and spirit.

On his arrival at Paris on 12 January 1797, Tone found a letter from his wife at Madgett's, dated from Hamburg and informing him of her safe arrival there about 20 December 1796, with Tone's sister, Mary, and the children. His brother, Matthew, had decided to settle in America. 'The transports of joy I felt at the news of her arrival were most dreadfully corrected by the accounts she gave me of her health, which threw me into the most terrible alarms. I wrote to her instantly to remain in Hamburg until further orders, and by no means to think of exposing herself in her present weak state, and our dear little babies, to a journey from Hamburg in this dreadful season, a great part of the road being through a wild country, where there is no better accommodation for travelling than open wagons.'

Her letter also gave the news of his sister's falling in love with a fellow-passenger, a young Swiss merchant called Giauque. With Tone's consent they mar-

ried and settled in Hamburg, 'so there is one more of
our family dispersed. I am sure that if there were five quarters of the globe, there would be one of us perched on the fifth.'

As before, he looked forward to living in retirement in some rural retreat. 'I am at present Adjutant-General, and I can live on my appointments,' he wrote to his wife, 'and when the peace comes, we will rent a cabin and a garden, and be as happy as Emperors on my half-pay.' He must have had a hardy constitution, for he told his wife that he was in the highest health, and should have been in as good spirits, save for the disquieting news of her health. He wrote thus after 'tossing three weeks on a stormy sea, and passing the last seven days in a carriage almost without sleep.' He was tormented by fears for her health. 'I am in a state of anxiety on your account which no words can express; I doat upon you; my life lies in you; I could not survive you four and twenty hours.'

General Hoche arrived in Paris on 21 January 1797, and a few days later was appointed to command the army of Sambre et Meuse. Tone applied to him to be allowed to retire from the service, preserving his pay and appointments, and offering his service at any time in the future. Hoche received this request very favourably, and recommended it to the Directory, who granted it without delay.

The old Tone spirit flashed out again when he saw in an English newspaper that in a debate in the Irish parliament, Fitzgibbon, now Earl of Clare, 'did me the favour to abuse me twice by name, as the father of the United Irishmen.... In the same debate, he called General Hoche a monster, so, at least, I had the pleasure to be abused in good company. I wrote a witty note, in an unknown language, which I please myself to call French, to the General thereupon, consoling him for the disgrace, etc., etc. I think I am

growing sprightly once more, but God knows the
heart!'

Late in February, he learned that he was to be
appointed to serve as Adjutant-General with the
army of Sambre et Meuse under General Hoche,
and that he would be attached to the General's staff,
to attend to his foreign correspondence.

His letters to his wife were taken up with advice to
her to guard her health and take the greatest possible
care of herself, and with hopes for their future happiness together, couched in optimistic terms. 'I came
here', he wrote to her, 'knowing not a single soul, and
scarcely a word of the language. I have the good fortune, so far, to obtain the confidence of the government, so far as was necessary for our affair, and to
secure the good opinion of my superior officers, as
appears by the station I hold. It is not every stranger
that comes into France and is made Adjutant-General.'

But to his Journal he confided his loneliness and
misery. 'I lead the life of a dog here in Paris, where I
am as much alone as in the deserts of Arabia. This
night, in downright wretchedness, I am come to a
tavern, where I write this memorandum in a little box
by myself. It is miserable. I wonder, shall I ever be so
happy as to see my dearest love and our little ones
once more. My mind is overgrown with docks and
thistles, for want of cultivation, and I cannot help it,
for I have not a soul to speak to whom I care a farth-
ing about. There are about half a dozen Irishmen here
in Paris that I have seen, but they are sad, vulgar
wretches, and I have been used to rather better company in all respects.'

A meeting with Thomas Paine broke the monotony
of his existence:

I have been lately introduced to the famous Thomas
Paine, and like him very well. He is vain beyond all

belief, but he has reason to be vain, and for my part I forgive him. He has done wonders for the cause of liberty, both in America and Europe, and I believe him to be conscientiously an honest man. He converses extremely well; and I find him wittier in discourse than in his writings, where his humour is clumsy enough. . . . I mentioned to him that I had known Burke in England, and spoke of his shattered state of mind, in consequence of the death of his only son, Richard. Paine immediately said that it was the *Rights of Man* which had broke his heart, and that the death of his son gave him occasion to develop the chagrin which had preyed upon him ever since the appearance of that work. I am sure the *Rights of Man* have tormented Burke exceedingly, but I have seen myself the workings of a father's grief on his spirit, and I could not be deceived. *Paine has no children.* Oh! my little babies, if I was to lose my Will, or my little Fantom! Poor little souls, I doat upon them, and on their darling mother, whom I love ten thousand times more than my own existence. They are never out of my thoughts. But to return to Paine. He drinks like a fish, a misfortune which I have known to befall other celebrated patriots. I am told that the true time to see him to advantage is about ten at night, with a bottle of brandy and water before him, which I can very well conceive.

His Journal goes on, 'Came home after dinner and sat some time alone, and devoured with the spleen. Opened my desk and read over all my dearest love's letters. They are my constant refuge, but latterly I am most terribly alarmed for her health. . . . Of all the privations I have suffered, that which I most sensibly feel, is the want of a friend since my arrival in France, to whom I could open my heart. If William, if Matt, if

Russell were here, what a difference it would make in my situation to-night. Well, I will go to my dreary bed; I declare I am weary of my existence.'

At length he received his orders to join the army, and expenses for the journey. A few days before he left, he received a letter from his sister 'which has thrown me into the greatest distress, I much fear that I shall lose my best beloved wife. I cannot write.' He left Paris on 29 March 1797 and arrived at Cologne on 7 April, all the time torn with anxiety about his wife. He then obtained Hoche's approval of his going to Hamburg, to open a channel of communication with Ireland, and to meet his wife.

Hoche asked Tone to assure his friends in Ireland that the French government, and Hoche personally, were bent on the emancipation of Ireland as much as ever, that preparations were on foot for a second attempt, and that it was a business that the Republic would never give up.

Hoche gave him no specific instructions, nor did he name any person that Tone should see in Hamburg. Tone recalled that 'George the Third, by the Grace of God, happens also to be Elector of Hanover' and he decided not to trust his person in George's dominions. He wrote to his family to meet him at Groningen on the Dutch side of Hanover. He set out from Cologne on 20 April, and finding that his family could not reach Groningen before 3 or 4 May, he passed a few days touring Holland. He was greatly taken by the neatness and good taste of the Dutch people, and of their houses and gardens, and gives a typically amusing account of his journey from Utrecht to Amsterdam in a trakschuyt:

a villainous barge, which is to the grand canal packet boat what a German postwagon is to a neat, well hung English chariot. The grand cabin, which is very small, being hired, I was stowed away amongst the common lumber. We were about thirty passengers, one half Jews, every man with his pipe in mouth. I was suffocated.... Opposite me was placed a fat Dutchman, with his mistress, I believe; so, to divert myself, and support the honour of the Republic, I determined to act the Celadon (lover) with Mademoiselle, who did not know one word of French. That did not, however, prevent me from making great way in her good graces, and Hans, who perceived he was losing ground fast, very wisely determined to renounce the contest, to which he found himself unequal, pulled his cap down over his eyes and composed himself to sleep. I laid my head down, without ceremony, in the lap of Mademoiselle, and in five minutes was as fast as a church. The lady followed the example of her two lovers, and, in this manner, at five in the morning we reached Amsterdam. I certainly had no right in the world to tease poor Hans; but, *Des Chevaliers Francais tel est le caractère;* besides, that he seemed *'not to be made of penetrable stuff'.* I will not venture to say as much of Mademoiselle, who, by-the-by, was very pretty.

He walked around the quays at Amsterdam, 'which are kept, as every thing else in Holland, with astonishing neatness'. He visited the Hague to see the Convention of the Batavian Republic in session. 'I have now seen the Parliament of Ireland, the Parliament of England, the Congress of the United States of America, the Corps Legislatif of France and the Convention Batave ... beyond all comparison the most shamelessly profligate and abandoned by all sense of virtue, principle or even common decency, was the legislature of my own unfortunate country; the scoundrels, I lose my temper every time I think of them.'

He arrived at Groningen on 2 May but had to wait until the 7th before his family joined him. 'I had the [113] unspeakable satisfaction to see my dearest love and our little babies, my sister and her husband, all arrive safe and well; it is impossible to describe the pleasure I felt.' In similar words did another exile, John Mitchel, set down his meeting in Van Diemen's Land with his wife after three years separation. 'Today I met my wife and family once more. These things cannot be described.'[24]

The Tone fortunes, as always, were shaky, and were not improved by the ineptitude of Dr Reynolds in Philadelphia. Instead of giving Mrs Tone specie in exchange for her stock, as Tone had instructed him to do, he gave her instead a bill on London for five hundred dollars. Tone now learned that this bill could not be collected. He wondered, too, that Mrs Tone had not received a letter from him, asking her to be sure to bring all his books and papers with her from America. This letter had been enclosed in one addressed to Reynolds and Rowan jointly, which they had received safely. Years later, when Tone's son, William, called on Dr Reynolds in Philadelphia and asked for his father's papers, Reynolds, then in the last stages of a fatal illness, could only show him an empty trunk. In this way, the Journals relating to three and a half years were lost.

The re-united family made a fortnight's tour of Holland and Belgium and then Tone rejoined Hoche's headquarters at Cologne. The family went on to Paris and settled in lodgings at Nanterre, where they had the Shees for neighbours. In a letter to his wife in early June, Tone wrote, 'Dear love, I look back on our last tour with the greatest delight. I never was, I think, so happy, and more happy I never can expect to be in future...'

While Tone was on his way to join his family,

Hoche had gained a great victory over the Austrians [114] in the battle of Neuwied. He was prevented from continuing his brilliant campaign to the gates of Vienna when Bonaparte opened peace negotiations at Loeben, a move which may have been inspired, partly at least, by the intense rivalry between these two ambitious generals. This was not unwelcome to Tone, for it turned Hoche's restless energy again to plans for a second attempt on Ireland.

Later, in June 1797, things began to move, and Tone was once more involved in the same anxious discussions and arguments that had preceded the Bantry Bay expedition. Edward Lewins, an authorised agent of the United Irishmen, had arrived at Hoche's headquarters from Hamburg, where he had been negotiating with Spanish and French agents. Hoche had immediately sent dispatches to the Directory and the Ministry of Marine, pressing for a new expedition, and had received a favourable response from both. The Ministry had decided that a large expedition should be sent. Tone knew from experience that this meant a delay of five or six months. He urged that a smaller fleet be organised with all speed to take advantage of the mutiny in the English navy. At Spithead the sailors had refused their duty until assured of better conditions. In great alarm, the Admiralty moved swiftly to meet their demands, but hardly had the men returned to their stations when trouble broke out in the ships at the Nore at the mouth of the Thames. This outbreak collapsed in a short time, and by early July, the Admiralty was in full control again.

Holland had been conquered by General Pichegru during the winter of 1794—5, and the Batavian Republic had been set up under French control. The serviceable Dutch fleet was now at the command of the French. Tone now learned from Hoche that the

Dutch were preparing an expedition against the English at the Texel. With Lewins, he set off for the Hague to confer with the Dutch commander-in-chief, General Daendels. When they met Hoche there, he told them that the Dutch, anxious to retrieve their national honour, had assembled sixteen ships of the line, ten frigates, and several transports, and intended to embark fifteen thousand troops, with arms and ammunition.

They were back at Hoche's headquarters at Cologne on 1 July 1797. Hoche had received orders to proceed to Paris. From there he intended to go to Brest, where, he told Tone, everything would be ready in a fortnight, and he hoped to be in Ireland in a month. The two young men parted with every expression of mutual liking and respect and with an optimism, which then seemed well-founded, as to the success of their plans.

On 8 July Tone arrived at the Texel, on the North Sea, and went on board Admiral de Winter's flagship, the *Vryheid*. He took an instant liking to both the Admiral and General Daendels. After he had seen the splendid condition of the fleet, far better than that at Brest, and had learned that the best possible spirit reigned in both soldiers and sailors, his spirits soared, and he wrote in his Journal, 'All is for the best in this best of all possible worlds.'

An English fleet under Admiral Duncan was on station off the Texel. Though he had received reinforcements after the ending of the mutinies, the Dutch still outnumbered him. But that faithful English ally, the wind, was not wanting. Tone's Journal tells the story.

17 July. The wind is as foul as the devil. At Brest we had, against all probability, a fair wind for five days consecutively, during all which time we were

not ready, and at last, when we did arrive at our destination, the wind changed and we missed our blow. Here all is ready and nothing is wanting but a fair wind. I hope the wind may not play us a trick. It is terribly foul this evening. Hang it and damn it for me! I am in a rage, which is truly astonishing, and can do nothing to help myself. Well! Well! 18 July. The wind is as foul as possible this morning; it cannot be worse. Hell! Hell! Hell! Allah! Allah! Allah! I am in a most devouring rage.

19 July. Wind foul still. Horrible. Horrible.

29 July. About mid-day the wind sprung up fresh, but the tide was spent and it was too late. To sail out of the Texel there must be a concurrence of wind and tide....

1, 2 August. Everything goes on here from bad to worse, and I am tormented and unhappy more than I can express, so that I hate even to make these memorandums....I am today twenty-five days aboard, and at a time when twenty-five hours are of importance. There seems to be a fate in this business. Five weeks, I believe six weeks, the English fleet was paralysed by the mutinies at Portsmouth, Plymouth and the Nore. The sea was open, and nothing to prevent both the Dutch and French fleets to put to sea. Well, nothing was ready; that precious opportunity, which we can never expect to return, was lost; and now that at last, we are ready here, the wind is against us, the mutiny is quelled and we are sure to be attacked by a superior force.

On 5 August, two United Irishmen from Co. Down, Lowry and Tennant, came aboard. Their news of the situation in Ireland was most disquieting. The harshest measures had been taken by the government, alarmed by the Bantry Bay expedition. The Protestant yeomanry and the militia had joined with the army under

General Lake in a campaign of terrorism. The Defenders and the United Irishmen had lost heart in large numbers at the failure of French aid to arrive.

The wind still continued foul at the Texel, and Tone rightly concluded that the chances of the expedition sailing as planned were rapidly receding. Provisions were running out, and the morale of the troops suffered as they remained crowded together on the vessels. Alternative plans were discussed, and a coolness developed between Admiral de Winter and General Daendels. Tone's heart sank as he saw the fatal disagreement between navy and army threaten to wreck the expedition finally and completely. However, early in September 1797, General Daendels proposed a major new plan. The troops should be disembarked ostentatiously, so as to delude the enemy that the expedition had been abandoned, but they would be quartered locally, so that they could be on board again in forty-eight hours. The ships would be re-victualled secretly. Then, when the enemy had relaxed his vigilance, the troops would be re-embarked with all speed and landed in Scotland. They would be followed by a second contingent of 15,000 French troops then in Dutch pay. Thirty thousand men could maintain themselves in Scotland in the face of any force that could be brought against them; twenty-five thousand might advance into England, and thus draw off troops from Ireland. This would present the remaining five thousand with the opportunity to cross to Ireland. Daendels gave Tone a copy of his memorial on this plan and dispatched him to Wetzlar, in Prussia, where Hoche now had his headquarters, to enquire whether he would take command of this expedition.

Tone arrived at Wetzlar on 12 September 1797, and was shocked by the appearance of Hoche, who had a dry, hollow cough, and seemed to Tone to be stricken with a rapid consumption. They discussed

Daendels' plan, and Hoche saw at once the weak
[118] points in it, but promised to consider it most carefully. It seemed to Tone that none of the general's
staff realised how serious his illness was, and Tone
had little faith in his physician. By 17 September,
Hoche could not walk and was carried from room to
room by four grenadiers. Tone wrote, 'It is terrible to
see a fine handsome fellow, in the very flower of his
youth and strength, so reduced. My heart bleeds for
him. I am told that the late attacks made on him by
the royalists in the convention, and the journalists in
their pay, preyed exceedingly on his spirits, and are
the probable cause of his present illness. Is it not
strange that a man who has faced death a thousand
times, with intrepidity in the field, should sink under
the calumny of a rabble of miscreants?'

Tone was referring to the coup d'etat of Fructidor,
in early September, when three of the Directory
carried out a purge, alleging a conspiracy to restore the
Bourbons. Barras, one of the Directors who plotted
the purge, had summoned Hoche to Paris in July with
part of the army, and named him Minister for War.
He was below the legal age for the post, and the troops'
route came closer to Paris than allowed by the constitution. Hoche, unaware of the real nature of the
intrigue, was hauled over the coals by the Directory,
while Barras sat silent and uttered not a word in his
defence, Hoche did not betray Barras, and returned
to the Army, sick in mind and body. Had he been in
good health, no doubt he would have shrugged off
this rebuff. He had endured more than one severe
winter campaign, but none could have been as wearing as the terrible voyage on board the *Fraternité*, wet
through most of the time, unable to snatch more than
a few hours sleep, and tormented by lack of news of
the rest of the fleet. Finally, there was the limping
return to France, and confirmation that the expedi-

tion had failed, a shattering set-back to a career marked until then by its dazzling successes. Even the brilliance of his victory at Neuwied had been clouded by Bonaparte's move, which prevented Hoche from gaining further laurels. Tone's alarm at his condition was only too well-founded. General Hoche died on 19 September 1797, at the age of twenty-nine.

That September was a black month for Tone and for Ireland. Carnot was a victim of the purge of Fructidor, and had fled for his life. He had been the moving spirit in the Directory urging on an invasion of Ireland, as Hoche had been the driving force in the army. Without them, the indomitable persistence of Tone faced a vacillating Directory that was to be swept aside by Bonaparte two years later.

The death of Hoche ended Tone's connection with the army of Sambre et Meuse and he set off for Paris the next day. He stayed a night at Bonn on the way, and with his friend Shee attended a grand fete to celebrate the anniversary of the founding of the French Republic. He dined in state with the Municipality, and drank sundry loyal and constitutional toasts, 'but not too many, as appears by this journal, which I am peacably writing at my inn. . . . I had promised a very pretty woman at dinner, whose name I know not, but whose person I reverence, to meet her to-night at a grand ball given by the Municipality, but I will deceive her like a false traitor, and go to my innocent bed; yet she is very pretty for all that, and speaks very pretty German French, and I am sure has not one grain of cruelty in her composition... Besides, I have just received a delightful letter from my dearest love, written three months ago, which has put me out of conceit with all women but herself, so, as before, I will go to my virtuous bed.'

He arrived in Paris about 1 October, and found his wife and family in good health and spirits. Lewins was also in Paris and all but acknowledged as Minister

from Ireland, 'and I am heartily glad of it: for I have an excellent opinion of his integrity and talents.' They went together to the Luxembourg to see Barras, and found him at home, giving favourable audience to his mistress, the voluptuous Madame Tallien, 'with whom he retired into an inner room, where they continued, I have no doubt, very seriously employed for about half an hour.' On his return, Tone presented General Daendels' plan to him. Barras listened attentively and referred them to the army authorities. Unfortunately, Scherer, the new Minister of War, detested the very name of Hoche, and, while professing interest, did nothing whatever.

Soon after Tone arrived in Paris, Admiral de Winter, under pressure from the Directory, put to sea, and on 11 October 1797, met an English fleet of almost equal size in the battle of Camperdown. The Dutch fleet was nearly annihilated. Tone noted wryly that by being sent on the mission to Hoche, he had escaped death or, at least, capture. 'It was well I was not on board the *Vryheid*. If I had, it would have been a pretty piece of business. I fancy I am not to be caught at sea by the English; for this is the second escape I have had and by land I mock myself of them'.

When the Treaty of Campo Formio was concluded later in October, the only enemies of the French that were left were England and Portugal. Paris celebrated with firing of cannon, bonfires and illuminations; Bonaparte's star was in the ascendant. Tone learned the next day of a decree dated 26 October creating the Army of England and appointing Bonaparte to command it. 'All this is famous news.' Pending the arrival of Bonaparte, the task of organising the new army was entrusted to General Desaix. Tone was presented to Desaix, who received him very favourably, and assured him that he was certain to be appointed to this army. 'So I may happen to have another offer at John Bull before I die. God knows how I deserve it.' [121]

This was all very well, but it was now nearly a year since the disaster of Bantry Bay, and no firm new plans concerning Ireland had emerged. Following the maxim of Dr Samuel Johnson's friend, that 'a dinner lubricates business', Tone, Lewins and some of the other Irishmen in Paris gave a dinner at Meot's, the celebrated restaurant which could offer patrons the choice of a hundred dishes. The guests of honour were Generals Desaix, Hedouville and Dufalga, with Watrin and Mermet, who had taken part in the Bantry Bay expedition. The dinner was superb and everything went off well. Fortunately, the next day Tone received his arrears of pay for four months.

In interviews with Desaix and Talleyrand, Minister for Foreign Affairs, Tone and Lewins were assured that the Directory remained committed to their cause and that all preparations would be complete by April 1798. Early in December, Bonaparte arrived in Paris. On 21 December Desaix presented Tone and Lewins to him at his house in the Rue Chantereine. Tone records the meeting:

He lives in the greatest simplicity, his house is small but neat, and all the furniture and ornaments in the most classical taste. He is about five feet six inches high, slender and well made, but stoops considerably; he looks at least ten years older than he is, owing to the great fatigues he underwent in his immortal campaign of Italy. His face is that of a profound thinker....

The meeting was indecisive; Bonaparte seemed to know little about Ireland. He asked them to call back and they saw him again on three occasions. At their last interview Lewins gave him a whole sheaf of papers relative to Ireland, including copies of several memo-[122] rials prepared by Tone nearly two years before. Tone put in a word for the refugee United Irishmen in Paris, and Bonaparte said that they would all be employed in the new army. For himself, Tone disclaimed any military competence, but hoped to be of service once they had crossed the water. 'But you are brave', interrupted Bonaparte. Tone noted that his manner was cold though he was perfectly civil. He spoke very little and was noncommital. It was impossible to augur anything good or bad from their talks with him.

To add to Tone's uneasiness, Napper Tandy had come to Paris and had instigated an intrigue against Tone and Lewins. It was with relief that Tone received his letters of service as Adjutant-General in the Army of England, with orders to report to headquarters at Rouen. He went with Lewins to take leave of Talleyrand and was gratified when the Foreign Minister assured them that the government held them in high regard. 'This is pleasant, the more so as poor Lewins and I have been tormented lately with dirty cabals and factions, which I scorn to commit to paper.' He attributed these attacks from other United Irishmen in Paris to jealousy of himself as Adjutant-General and of Lewins as being received as virtually an ambassador.

Tone was shattered to learn on 26 March of the arrest in Dublin of the Leinster Directory of the United Irishmen, including Thomas Addis Emmet, Bond and McNevin, and that warrants had been issued for the arrest of Lord Edward Fitzgerald and others. He suspected treachery. The mortifying truth was that his friends had been betrayed by Thomas Reynolds, the husband of his wife's sister.

These events sharpened his impatience to join another expedition, but soon after his arrival at Rouen on 5 April it became clear that Bonaparte had turned his attention to the East. In fact, he had made a lightning inspection of the French western ports with General Desaix in March. Contemptuous of the lack of progress, he had abandoned the idea of an assault on England. Later in April the Paris newspapers announced that Bonaparte had taken command of an expedition to Egypt and Syria. It was conjectured that Palestine would be restored to the Jews, who would reward the French from their immense wealth. Tone reflected ruefully that Ireland seemed but a pawn in these great affairs. 'What miserable pygmies we unfortunate Irish are!'

A last gleam of sunshine strikes out from his Journal for May 1798. 'Having obtained leave of absence for two decades, I have spent the last twenty days deliciously with my family at Paris.' His happiness was increased by good news of his family. A letter from his brother William, dated sixteen months before from Poona, said that he was second-in-command of the infantry of the Mahratta State, at a salary of £750 a year. This was a remarkable achievement for a young man who had gone out to India as a private soldier. Matthew had arrived in Paris in November 1797, and now there was news from the youngest brother, Arthur, aged sixteen, that he was on his way to Paris from Hamburg. Tone managed to obtain a commission in the French navy for Matthew, and Arthur obtained one in the Dutch navy. The coming together of the family after long separation seemed to Tone to be a happy augury for the future.

A diversion came at the end of May. The English were bombarding Le Havre from the sea and Tone was ordered there to assist in the defence. He was stationed in a shore battery and came under fire. 'It was a fine sight and I should have enjoyed it more, had it not been for certain speculations on futurity

and the transmigration of souls which presented themselves to my fancy at times.'

A conversation with General Kilmaine in mid June could not have been gloomier. The French navy was in a worse state of disorganisation than before, without money, without stores, without ammunition and with ships completely unfit to put to sea. On the heels of this came news from Ireland of the arrest and death of Lord Edward Fitzgerald, and of the outbreak of insurrection in several counties of Leinster.

He returned to Rouen on 19 June and there met General Grouchy who had been appointed to command the cavalry of the Army of England. They relived the frustrations of Bantry Bay. Grouchy regretted that he had not seized Bouvet by the collar and thrown him overboard the moment he attempted to raise a difficulty as to the landing. He pleased Tone by his professed zeal to mount another expedition and talk of going to Paris to press the Directory to move. It is strange that Tone, after the event, at no time blamed Grouchy. His son, William, was forthright in his condemnation of 'the indecision of Grouchy, of that honest but wavering man who twice held the fate of Europe in his hands, at Bantry Bay and at Waterloo, and twice let it slip through them, from want of resolution.'[25]

From Grouchy he went to General Kilmaine, and burst into a rage when told that the Directory had decided to postpone another invasion until a more favourable occasion. Unless French help was sent soon, it would be too late. Kilmaine answered that the Directory were unable to mount a large expedition and unwilling to risk a small one. Now Tone felt the loss of Hoche. 'If he were alive, he would be in Ireland in a month, if he went only with his staff in a fishing boat.' Angrily he said to Kilmaine that 5,000 men who could be sent were better than 50,000 that

could not. He obtained leave to go to Paris in view of
the news from Ireland.

His Journal ends on 30 June 1798 with a perplexed
paragraph on the apparent lack of action in the North
in the insurrection. 'What can be the cause of their
passive submission, at this moment, so little suited to
their former zeal and energy? I remember what Digges
said to Russell and me, five or six years ago — if ever
the South is roused I would rather have one Southerner
than twenty Northerners — Digges was a man of great
sense and observation. He was an American and had
no local or provincial prejudices. Was he right in his
opinion? A very little time will let us see. If it should
prove so, what a mortification to me, who have so long
looked up with admiration to the North, and especially
to Belfast. It cannot be that they have changed their
principles; it must be, that circumstances render all
exertions on their part, as yet, impossible.'

8

Homecoming

Tone and Lewins had received disjointed and incomplete reports of the situation in Ireland during 1797 and the early months of 1798. Alarming though they were, these reports did not reflect the full horror of the government's repressive measures, which were enforced with a savagery that eventually led to the rising in Wexford.

The main plank in the policy administered from Dublin Castle was the maintenance of the Protestant ascendancy. In Ulster this was achieved by a campaign directed against the United Irishmen, while Orangemen were enrolled into the yeomanry and allowed to act as magistrates. Flogging, half-hanging and the pitch-cap were freely used to extract information about arms held by United Irishmen and Defenders. By the end of 1797 this campaign, led by the ferocious General Lake, had succeeded in 'pacifying' Ulster. It was the peace of exhaustion.

The leaders of the United Irishmen in Dublin determined that the time had come to rise in rebellion. They fixed on 23 May 1798. The movement was riddled with informers. As Tone had learned, the Leinster Directory had been seized in March, and in June Lord Edward Fitzgerald had died from wounds received when being arrested. At the end of March martial law was proclaimed. The military, yeomanry and militia were let loose on the countryside and began a reign of terror with burning of homesteads, summary executions and floggings. Wexford rose in late May and at first a rebel army of pikemen carried all before them. They captured Wexford and Enniscorthy, and General Sir John Moore wrote in his diary that if the rebellion continued or the French came, the country was lost. Twenty thousand insurgents faced General Lake's army on Vinegar Hill. But the French did not come and the Wexfordmen were defeated. Pikes were no match for cannon.

Early in June, Ulster rose and 6,000 United Irishmen under Henry Joy McCracken attacked Antrim town. In Down, Henry Munro led 7,000 men, at first with some success, but was overwhelmingly defeated in the battle of Ballinahinch. The outbreak was quelled within a week. McCracken and Munro were hanged.

Tone and Lewins continued to press the Directory to send aid, hoping that it would arrive in time. In July the French agreed to send three expeditions, under Generals Humbert, Hardy and Kilmaine. The first two were to start simultaneously, Humbert with 1,000 men and Hardy with the main army of 3,000. All going well, Kilmaine was to follow with a force of 9,000 men.

Again, incompetence, lack of funds and ill-fortune combined to defeat a plan that gave reasonable prospect of success, even granted that the rising in Ireland had been virtually put down by then. Humbert did not sail until 6 August. His brief and extraordinary campaign sheds a romantic aura around the otherwise fearful story of the '98 rising. He landed at Killala, Co. Mayo, on 23 August, and four days later chased General Lake's troops out of Castlebar, the defeated garrison dropping their arms and fleeing all the way to Tuam in the famous 'Races of Castlebar'. A local Catholic gentleman, John Moore, was appointed President of Connaught. But Humbert waited in vain for the arrival of Hardy with reinforcements, and on 8

September his small force surrendered to a vastly superior army under Cornwallis at Ballinamuck. The French were treated as prisoners-of-war but the Irish who had rallied to their standard were slaughtered without mercy. Matthew Tone and Bartholomew Teeling, officers on Humbert's staff, were tried in Dublin by court martial and hanged.

Meanwhile, Tone had joined Hardy's staff at Brest. Again he had the mortification of seeing the vital days slip away while Hardy waited first for money to pay his men and buy stores, and then for a favourable wind. Brest still harboured many English spies and a well, the Paris newspapers published descriptions of the preparations. The English even knew that Tone was on Hardy's staff. When Hardy eventually sailed on 16 September the English fleet was soon in pursuit. Hardy's fleet consisted of seven frigates, a schooner and as flagship the *Hoche*, a ship of the line. They carried 3,000 troops. By 10 October he had reached the coast of Donegal. That evening his fleet was sighted by the English under Sir John Warren. The wind had risen to gale force, but on the morning of the 12th the English closed in to the attack. Tone was on board the *Hoche*. When a boat came alongside from the schooner asking for orders, the French Admiral Bompard and his officers urged Tone to go on board the schooner, which would have a better chance to outsail pursuers than the slow flagship. 'Our contest is hopeless,' they said. 'We will be prisoners-of-war, but what will become of you?' He declined, saying 'Shall it be said of me that I fled whilst the French were fighting the battles of my country?'[26]

A fierce sea-battle ensued and the superior English fleet was victorious. The *Hoche* fought furiously for four hours until she was a dismasted wreck, her guns silenced. Tone commanded a battery on the gun deck and according to French reports, fought with the utmost desperation, as if he were courting death.

The weather continued so stormy that it was three weeks before the captured ship could be brought into Lough Swilly. When Tone stepped ashore, he immediately recognised and saluted Sir George Hill who had been a fellow student at Trinity College. He was put in irons and sent to Dublin for trial. He protested that he was an officer in the French army, as proved by his papers, and claimed the rights and privileges of a prisoner-of-war, but without avail. He was escorted into Dublin on 8 November, sitting in a carriage and dressed in the brilliant uniform of a French colonel, a large cocked hat with broad gold lace, blue uniform coat with gold and embroidered collar and gold epaulettes, blue pantaloons and short boots bound with gold lace. His legs were in irons. He was lodged in the Provost's Prison and brought up before a court martial on 10 November, still wearing his French uniform. His trial aroused great public excitement and the courtroom was crowded. The charge was read, that he had acted traitorously against the King, to whom, as a natural-born subject, he owed all allegiance. Tone admitted all the charges, and asked permission to read a statement explaining the reasons and motives of his conduct. Permission was given, provided he confined himself within the bounds of moderation.

His statement, a vindication of his revolutionary career, makes moving reading. He began with his belief that the connection between Ireland and Great Britain was the curse of the Irish nation. To break that connection, he had sought the aid of the French Republic. Attached to no party there, without interest, without money, without intrigue, he had won the confidence of the French Directory, the approbation of its generals and the esteem and affection of his comrades. To liberate his country, he had encountered the chances of war among strangers and on the seas dominated by the ships of war of England. He had left a beloved wife unprotected, and children whom he adored, fatherless. After such sacrifices, it was no great effort to add that of his life.

He went on to lament the atrocities that had been committed on both sides. His design had been to attain freedom by fair and open war. He had been absent from Ireland for four years and no responsibility for such horrors could be attributed to him. After a combat nobly sustained, he had been brought to Dublin in irons like a felon, to the eternal disgrace of those who gave the order. Whatever the sentence of the court, he was prepared for it; 'its members will surely discharge their duty; I shall take care not to be wanting in mine.' He then made a last request, that he should be shot as a soldier, and cited the precedent of the French emigrés.

He was taken back to prison, escorted by the notorious Major Sandys, whose kindness he acknowledges in his last letter to his father. Sir John Moore wrote that he had conducted himself with great firmness and manliness. An old friend, William Sinclair of Belfast, was at the trial and reported that Tone had behaved perfectly like a gentleman and a brave man. The Marquis of Buckingham was also present and wrote to his brother, Lord Grenville, with an account of the trial, ending with a statement which reads prophetically in the light of events. 'Notwithstanding all this, he was much agitated and I cannot help thinking that he means to destroy himself before Monday, on which day it is supposed he will be hanged.'[27]

Monday 12 November was indeed the day set for his execution by the public hangman. Lord Cornwallis, the Lord Lieutenant, had refused his request to be shot. In prison on the evening of the trial, Tone wrote to the Directory, the Minister of Marine,

General Kilmaine, Mr Shee in France and several of his friends in Ireland, on behalf of his family. To his father he wrote that he had declined to see him since he had not the courage to support a meeting which could lead to nothing and would put them both to insupportable pain. To his wife he wrote:

Dearest Love,

The hour is at last come when we must part. As no words can express what I feel for you and our children, I shall not attempt it; complaint of any kind would be beneath your courage and mine; be assured I will die as I have lived and that you will have no cause to blush for me.

I have written on your behalf to the French government, to the Minister of Marine, to General Kilmaine, and to Mr Shee; with the latter I wish you especially to advise. In Ireland I have written to your brother Harry and to those of my friends who are about to go into exile and who I am sure will not abandon you.

Adieu, dearest love: I find it impossible to finish this letter. Give my love to Mary; and above-all things remember that you are now the only parent of our dearest children and that the best proof you can give of your affection for me will be to preserve yourself for their education. God Almighty bless you all.

Yours ever,
T. W. Tone

P.S. I think you have a friend in Wilson, who will not desert you.

The following evening, the 11th, he wrote to her again.

Dearest Love,

I write just one line, to acquaint you that I have

received assurances from your brother Edward, of his determination to render every assistance and protection in his power; for which I have written to thank him most sincerely. Your sister has likewise sent me assurances of the same nature, and expresssed a desire to see me, which I have refused, having determined to speak to no one of my friends, not even my father, from motives of humanity to them and myself. It is a very great consolation to me, that your family are determined to support you; as to the manner of that assistance, I leave it to their affection for you, and your own excellent good sense, to settle what manner will be most respectable for all parties.

Adieu, dearest love. Keep your courage, as I have kept mine; my mind is as tranquil this moment as at any period of my life. Cherish my memory; and, especially, preserve your health and spirits for the sake of our dearest children.

Your ever affectionate,
T. Wolfe Tone

That same evening, he was told that he was to be publicly hanged the following day, Monday, 12 November. Early that Monday morning, he cut his throat from ear to ear, partly severing the windpipe. The weapon used was a razor, apparently left by his brother Matthew, who had been taken out to be hanged from the same cell.[28] A surgeon was called in, and reported that as Tone had missed the jugular vein, the wound was not fatal, but extremely dangerous. He bound up the prisoner's neck, and said that to move him would be fatal. When told that he might yet survive, Tone murmured 'I am sorry I have been so bad an anatomist.'

Meanwhile, his lawyer friends, Curran and Burrowes, made an attempt to delay the execution. They applied to the King's Bench for a writ of *habeas corpus,* arguing that a military court could not have juris- [133] diction over a civil prisoner while the Court of King's Bench was sitting, and that Tone was not a member of the Crown forces. The Lord Chief Justice was Lord Kilwarden, formerly Arthur Wolfe, who as Attorney-General had helped to save Tone during the Jackson affair. He ordered that the writ be prepared and sent the Sheriff to the prison to stop the execution. The Sheriff brought back the news of Tone's attempted suicide and the surgeon gave evidence that to move him would be fatal.

Tone lingered on for a week, alone, forbidden by the surgeon to move or speak. On the morning of 19 November he stirred on his bed with a spasm of approaching death. 'Keep still,' the surgeon warned him, 'the slightest movement will be fatal.' Tone whispered, 'I can yet find words to thank you, sir; it is the most welcome news you could give me. What should I wish to live for?' With these words he died. He was thirty-five years old.

There were rumours that he was murdered by his captors to avoid surrendering him to the court. But surely they would have found more efficient means to dispatch him and avoided the risk of denunciation by a victim who was only wounded, however grievously. They clearly intended to defy the court and proceed with the public hanging. And Tone had made up his mind long before, that, if captured, he would not submit to that indignity. His son records that at a dinner in Paris, with his wife present, he made his attitude clear, some months before sailing from Brest. Taking his own life in those circumstances was not suicide, in his opinion, but simply choosing the mode of his death. His family considered him a martyr. 'His death can never be considered as a suicide', wrote his son. 'It was merely the resolution of a noble mind to disappoint, by his own act, the brutal ferocity of his enemies, and avoid the indignity of their touch.'[29] It was so regarded by Lucien Bonaparte, when he addressed the Council of Five Hundred on behalf of Tone's widow and children.[30]

His body was given to his relatives and was buried, it is believed, in the grave of his grandfather in the churchyard at Bodenstown. This is now the scene of annual pilgrimages by different groups, all claiming to be the legitimate inheritors of his republican aspirations. He left his pocket-book to a friend, John Sweetman. It was stained with blood and he had written on the lining the date, 11 November, and a quotation from Virgil's Second Eclogue, 'Te nunc habet ista secundum.' It is now in the National Museum. His death mask is in his old college, Trinity, Dublin.

His widow, Matilda, suffered further heavy sorrows in the death of their daughter Maria from consumption in 1802 at sixteen, and of their son Francis from the same disease in 1806 at the age of thirteen. Inadequate financial support from the French government in the early years of her widowhood was supplemented by assistance from Thomas Wilson, of Dullatur, Scotland, whom she had met on board ship from America in 1796, and who indeed proved a good friend, as Tone had foretold. They were married in 1816 and settled in America, at Georgetown, D.C., with her surviving son, William. Wilson died in 1824, and William Tone in 1828. Widowed for the second time, and having watched all her children die, she lived on with her memories until 1849.

Tone's closest friend, Thomas Russell, tried to organise Ulster for Robert Emmet, was arrested, tried for high treason, and hanged at Downpatrick on 21 October 1803.

Tone has been hailed as the father of Irish republicanism. The memorial over his grave is inscribed with words written by Patrick Pearse: '. . . to his teach-ing we owe it that there is such a thing as Irish [135] Nationalism and to the memory of the deed he nerved his generation to do, to the memory of '98 we owe it that there is any manhood left in Ireland.'

He was twenty-six before he appeared to take more than a passing interest in politics or public affairs. As undergraduate student at the Middle Temple in Lon-don and fledgling barrister, he showed indolence, high spirits and susceptibility to pretty women. An obituary notice in *Faulkner's Dublin Journal* said that his com-pany was coveted by every student of taste in the University.[31]

His first pamphlet can fairly be described as a flexing of his polemical muscles. His second raised the question of Ireland's right to remain neutral when England went to war, and foreshadowed his later view that Irish independence was not incompatible with loyalty to the King as King of Ireland.

His third pamphlet, his best and most famous, *An Argument on Behalf of the Catholics of Ireland*, appeared in 1791. It was his nature, once convinced of the justice of a cause, to espouse it wholeheartedly. And so it was with the Catholic cause. He was bitterly disappointed at the pusillanimity of Keogh and the others who failed miserably to ram home the advan-tage gained by the petition to the King. He would have been consoled by the considered judgment of Lecky that the Catholic Relief Bill of 1793 was infinitely more important than O'Connell's Emancipa-tion of 1829.[32] Tone's tireless energy, his ability as a pamphleteer and his complete dedication to the Catholic cause must be given a large share of the credit for the relief obtained.

The Jackson affair showed how, possibly subcon-sciously, he had moved to a position that can only be described as that of a revolutionary. It seems that it

was only after he had given Rowan his paper on the
favourable prospects for a French invasion that he
himself realised how far he had gone (although his
Journals give the erroneous impression that his political views were fully developed from the time he
wrote his first pamphlet). After that, there could be
no turning back. His exile to America clearly embit-
tered him, and hardened him in his view that England's
lordship of Ireland must be overthrown. From then
on, he worked with single-minded determination
towards one objective, to free his country with the
help of the French.

At this remove, it is easy to see how badly organised
the United Irishmen were. In trusting informers like
McNally and Reynolds, they showed astonishing
naïvety. Tone can be faulted for misleading the French
concerning the situation in Ireland, and for failing to
ensure that his friends in Ireland were kept informed
of the French expeditions, that to Bantry Bay in particular. In the event, of course, it was the failure to
land French forces in sufficient strength that lost the
day. He failed, and the United Irishmen failed. But
the republican and democratic principles that Tone
propagated and the political creed and tradition of
the United Irishmen continue to influence Irish men
and women to the present day.

What can one say of the man himself? Few revolu-
tionaries have written so frankly about themselves.
He confessed that he loved fame. He made no secret
of his ambition to take a high and honoured place in
a free Ireland, nor of his conviction that such honour
would be his due. He could never have been satisfied
to pass his life as a comfortable and conforming
lawyer. His judgment of men was sometimes very
faulty, as in his high regard for Digges and Grouchy.
His own circumstances, desperate at times, and the
circumstances of his day, combined with his tempera-

ment to lead him on the path which brought him, in the end, to the Provost's Prison. But his gaiety, his self- mockery and his courage must endear him to all who read his story. Pearse spoke for them when he said at Bodenstown, 'I do not ask you to venerate him as a saint; I ask you to love him as a man.'[33]

References

1. Lecky, *A History of Ireland in the Eighteenth Century*, vol. II, 182.
2. *Dublin University Calendar, 1941—42*, 1.
3. Barrington, *Personal Sketches of his Own Times*, vol. I, 153.
4. Madden, *The United Irishmen: Their Lives and Times*, 2nd ed, vol. II, 142.
5. Tone MSS, Trinity College, Dublin.
6. *Trial between Richard Martin and John Petrie, reported by a student of the Temple*, Dublin 1792.
7. Tone MSS.
8. Burrowes Papers, Royal Irish Academy, 25K53.
9. Walsh, *Sketches of Ireland Sixty Years Ago*, 2nd ed, 137—8.
10. Russell Papers, State Paper Office, Dublin.
11. Chatham Papers, Public Record Office, London.
12. This letter was not published by *Faulkner's Dublin Journal* which was strongly pro-government. Tone's son published it for the first time in his *Life* of his father, vol. I, 495.
13. Russell Papers.
14. Chatham Papers.
15. ibid.
16. Russell Papers.
17. This conflicts with Tone's statement in May 1795 that when leaving for America he had only £700 in money and bills on Philadelphia. He may have received funds meanwhile from friends in Ireland.
18. Tone MSS.
19. Croker, *Popular Songs Illustrative of the French Invasion of Ireland*, parts III and IV.
20. *The New Cambridge Modern History*, vol. IX, chap. XI, 315.
21. Desbrière, Capitaine E. *Projets et Tentatives de Debarquement aux Iles Britannique*, tome I, 213.

22. Shannon MSS, National Library of Ireland, 13, 303.
23. Yeats, W. B., 'The Ghost of Roger Casement', *Collected Poems*, 352, London 1978. [139]
24. Mitchel, John, *Jail Journal*, 259, Dublin n.d.
25. Tone, T. W., *Life of . . . Written by Himself and continued by his Son*, vol. II, 511.
26. ibid., vol. II, 523.
27. Correspondence of William Grenville, vol. IV, London 1905.
28. *Freeman's Journal*, 13 November 1798.
29. Tone, op. cit. vol. II, 540.
30. ibid., vol. II, 554.
31. *Faulkner's Dublin Journal*, 22 November 1798.
32. Lecky, op. cit., vol. III, 148.
33. Pearse, P. H., oration at Bodenstown, 22 June 1913.

Select Bibliography

Manuscript Sources

Trinity College, Dublin: Tone manuscripts, including incomplete autobiography and journal. Some passages were omitted by his son from the *Life*

State Paper Office, Dublin: The Russell Papers

Royal Irish Academy, Dublin: The Burrowes Papers

Public Record Office, London: The Chatham Papers

National Library of Ireland: Shannon MSS

Newspapers

Faulkner's Dublin Journal

Freeman's Journal

Books and Pamphlets

Barrington, Sir Jonah, *Personal Sketches of his Own Times*, London 1869

Beckett, J. C., *The Anglo-Irish Tradition*, London 1976

Craig, M. J., *Dublin 1660–1860*, London 1952

Croker, Thomas Crofton, *Popular Songs Illustrative of the French Invasions of Ireland*, Printed for the Percy Society, London 1847

de Latocnaye, *Promenade d'un Français dans l'Irlande (1796–97)*, Dublin 1797

Desbrière, E., Capitaine, *Projets et Tentatives de Debarquement aux Iles Britannique*, Paris 1900

Dowling, V., *Proceedings of Trial of Wolfe Tone*, Dublin 1798 (Joly Pamphlets)

Drennan, W., *The Drennan Letters*, ed. D. A. Chart, Belfast 1931

Fitzpatrick, W. J., *Secret Service under Pitt*, London 1892.

Hayes, Richard, *The Last Invasion of Ireland*, Dublin 1937.

Hobson, Bulmer, *Letters of Wolfe Tone*, Dublin n.d.

Howell, T. B. and T. J., eds., *State Trials*, vols XXII to XXVII, London 1811–26

Jacob, R., *The Rise of the United Irishmen 1791−1794*, London 1937

Jones, Commander E. Stuart, R.N., *An Invasion that Failed*, London 1950

Lecky, W. E. H., *A History of Ireland in the Eighteenth Century*, 5 vols, London 1892−96

Madden R. R., *The United Irishmen, their Lives and Times*, 4 vols, Dublin 1857−60

Mahan, Alfred Thayer, *Influence of Sea Power upon the French Revolution and Empire*, 2 vols, London 1893

Maxwell, Constantia, *A History of Trinity College, Dublin 1591−1892*, Dublin 1946

Moore, Sir John, *Diary*, ed. Sir J. F. Maurice, London 1904

Morgan, Edward, 'A Journal of the Movements of the French Fleet in Bantry Bay from their first appearance to their final departure', reproduced in the Cork Historical and Archaeological Society's *Journal*, vol. XXI, 2nd series, 1915

MacDermot, Frank, *Theobald Wolfe Tone and His Times*, London 1939

McDowell R. B., 'The personnel of the Dublin society of United Irishmen 1791−4', *Irish Historical Studies*, ii, 12−53

McDowell R. B., *Irish Public Opinion 1750−1800*, London 1944

MacManus, M. J., *A Bibliography of Theobald Wolfe Tone*, Dublin 1940

O'Faolain, Sean, ed., *Autobiography of Wolfe Tone*, London 1937

Paine, Thomas, *Rights of Man, Being an Answer to Mr Burke's Attack on the French Revolution*, London 1791

Pearse, P. H., *Tracts for the Times, No. 11, The Separatist Idea*, Dublin 1916.

Tone, Theobald Wolfe, *Life of... Written by Himself and continued by his Son; with his Political Writings and Fragments of his Diary ...* ed. William T. W. Tone, 2 vols., Washington 1826

Trial between Richard Martin and John Petrie, reported by a student of the Temple, Dublin 1792.

Wall, Maureen, *The Penal Laws*, Dublin Historical Association, Dundalk 1961

Walsh J. E., *Ireland Sixty Years Ago*, Dublin 1847

Young, Arthur, *A Tour in Ireland*, ed. A. W. Hutton, 2 vols., London 1892

Index

Adet, Citizen (French Minister in Philadelphia), 55, 59, 65
Aherne, (United Irishman), 78, 79, 81
Altamont, Lord, 30
Anderson, (Trinity College undergraduate), 5

Ballinamuck, battle of, 128
Barras, 118, 120
Barrington, Sir Jonah, 5, 43
Barry, Colonel H., 29
Bedout, Captain, 97, 99
Bellew, Christopher, 32
Beresford, John, 44, 48
Beresford, Marcus, 44
Bodenstown, Co. Kildare, 2, 8, 11, 134, 137
Bompard, Admiral, 128
Bonaparte, Lucien, 134
Bonaparte, Napoleon, 67, 78, 81, 114, 119–23
Bond, Oliver, 22, 36, 84, 122
Bouvet, Admiral, 89, 91, 93–7, 99, 106, 124
Braughall, Tom, 30
Bridport, Admiral, 99, 102
Browne, Denis, 30
Bruce, Rev. William, 20
Bruix, (naval chief-of-staff to Bantry Bay expedition), 92
Buckingham, Marquis of, 130
Burke, Edmund, 5, 15, 33, 110
Burke, Richard, 26, 29, 110
Burrowes, Peter, 15, 132
Burton, Beresford, 27
Bushe, Charles Kendal, 5
Butler, Simon, 21, 23, 27, 36, 37
Byrne, Edward, 'The Vintner', 26, 32, 34, 48
Byrne, Patrick, 10, 14

Camperdown, battle of, 120
Carnot, Lazare, 68–71, 76, 79, 81, 82, 86, 119
Castlebar, Co. Mayo, 127
Catholic Committee, 24–5, 31, 36, 37, 39, 44, 46, 73, 74–5, 78
Catholic Relief Act, 1793, 34–5
Cave Hill, Belfast, 51
Cherin, General, 82, 89, 93, 94, 95
Chudleigh, Elizabeth, 42
Clare, Earl of, see Fitzgibbon, John
Clarke, General, 71, 75–82, 86
Cochrane, Captain Lord, 54
Cockayne, John, 42, 43, 45, 46, 49
Colpoys, Admiral, 89, 99, 102
Cook, Captain, 10
Cornwallis, Lord, 128, 130
Craig, Rev., 2, 3
Croker, Thomas Crofton, 104
Curran, John Philpot, 49, 132

Daendels, General, 115, 117, 120
Dalrymple, General, 102, 103
Darling, Sisson, 2
D'Aucourt, M., 63, 64, 70
Defenders, 28, 36, 40, 73, 75, 92
Delacroix, Charles, 65, 66, 70, 71, 75, 78, 79
Desaix, General, 120, 121, 123
Desbrière, Captain E., 105
Devereux, James, 32, 33
de Winter, Admiral, 115, 117, 120
Digges, Thomas, 15, 16, 17, 36, 125, 136
Drennan, Dr William, 15, 17, 19, 20, 27, 46
Duncan, Admiral, 115
Dundas, Henry, 32

East India Company, 2, 9, 10

Emmet, Robert, 15, 134
Emmet, Thomas Addis, 15, 22, 49, 50, 51, 122

Fanning, Edward, 8, 11, 14
Faulkner's Dublin Journal, 39, 135
Fingall, Lord, 25
Fitzgerald, Lord Edward, 22, 62, 80, 103, 122, 124, 126
Fitzgibbon, John, Earl of Clare, 33, 36, 37, 39, 40, 46, 47, 48, 70, 72, 78, 108
Fitzsimons, Father, 76
Fitzwilliam, Lord, 47, 48
French Dr, Bishop of Elphin, 30
French, Sir Thomas, 32, 34

George III, 1, 32, 33, 36, 37, 47, 111
Giauque, M., 2, 107
'Gog', *see* Keogh, John
Gormanston, Lord, 25
Grattan, Henry, 12, 13, 28, 29, 48
Grenville, Lord, 15, 130
Griffith, Richard, 8
Grouchy, General, 88, 91–6, 99, 100, 105, 107, 124, 136

Hall, John, 9
Hamill, Roger, 48
Hamilton, Sackville, 46
Hardy, General, 127, 128
Hervey, Hon. Augustus, 42
Hill, Sir George, 129
Hobart, Robert, 34, 36
Hoche, General Lazare, 67, 81–6, 88, 89, 93, 96, 100, 101, 103, 108, 109, 111, 113, 114, 115, 117–19, 120, 124
Hope, Jemmy, 22
Humbert, General, 103, 127, 128
Hutton, Mr (nickname for Tone), 20

Jackson, Rev. William, 41–5, 46, 48, 49, 55, 135
James II, 3, 4
Johnson, Dr Samuel, 121
Jones, Todd, 37

'Keeper of the College Lions, The,' *see* Stokes, Whitley
Kenmare, Lord, 25
Keogh, John, 'Gog', 19, 25–7, 29, 32, 34, 40, 48, 51, 58, 59, 78, 103

Kilmaine, General, 124, 127, 131
Kilwarden, Lord, *see* Arthur Wolfe
Kingston, Duke of, 42
Knox, George, 9, 28, 39, 44, 51

Lake, General Gerard, 117, 126, 127
Lamport, Captain, 1
Lawless, John, 22
Lecky, W. E. H., 4, 135
Le Havre, 60–63
Leonard, Captain, 57
Lepaux, Le Reveilliere, 68
Lewins, E. J., 92, 114, 115, 119, 121, 122, 126, 127
Louis XVI, 33, 34
Lowry (United Irishman), 116

McCormick, Richard, 'Magog', 26, 27, 41, 51, 59
McCracken, Henry Joy, 51, 52, 127
McDonnell, James, 53
McDonnell, R., 34
McNally, Leonard, 42–3, 44, 49, 136
McNevin, William, 22, 122
Madgett, Nicholas, 42, 66, 68, 70, 75, 76, 77, 79, 81, 107
Magee, Archbishop, 5, 70
'Magog', *see* McCormick, Richard
Martin, Mrs, 6, 7
Martin, Richard, 6, 7
Moira, Francis Rawdon, 1st Earl, 29
Moira, Lady, 29
Monroe, James, 64, 65, 68, 70
Moore, General Sir John, 127, 130
Moore, John, 127
Morard de Galles, Admiral, 84, 88, 90, 91, 100, 101, 104
Moylan, Dr, Bishop of Cork, 31
Munro, Henry, 127

Napoleon, *see* Bonaparte
Neilson, Samuel, 19, 28, 51, 52, 59, 84, 103
Norbury, Lord, *see* Toler, John

O'Connor, Arthur, 22, 80, 103
O'Flynn, Captain O'Byrne, 55

Paine, Thomas, 1, 16, 19, 109–10
Parsons, Sir Lawrence, afterwards Earl of Rosse, 13

Pearse, Patrick H., 135, 137

[144] 'Peep o' Day Boys', 28

Pellew, Captain Edward, 89, 90, 91

Penal Laws, 4

Petrie, John, 7

Phipps, Benjamin, 9, 10

Pichegru, General, 67, 114

Pitt, William, 10, 14, 37, 42, 45–8

Pius VI, Pope, 81

Plunket, James, 30

Plunket, William, 5, 70

Ponsonby, George, 12, 13, 24, 46, 49

'P.P., Clerk of this Parish', *see* Russell, Thomas

Rawdon, General, Lord, 29, 32, 40

Reynolds, Dr, 55, 59, 79, 113

Reynolds, Thomas, 122, 136

Richmond, Duke of, 15

Robespierre, Maximilien, 55

Roche, Sir Boyle, 26

Rowan, Archibald Hamilton, 21, 22, 23, 31, 43, 44, 45, 46, 55, 59, 60, 65, 79, 82, 113

Russell, Thomas, 'P.P. Clerk of this Parish', 14–20, 28, 29, 36, 41, 49, 50, 51, 56–7, 58, 59, 66, 67, 68, 84, 103, 111, 125

Sandys, Major, 130

Scherer (French Minister for War), 120

Secret Committee of House of Lords, 36–7

Shannon, Lord, 106

Sheares, the brothers Henry and John, 22

Shee, Colonel, 83, 84, 86, 113, 119, 131

Siddons, Sarah, 9

Simms (two brothers), 51, 52, 58, 59

Sinclair, William, 130

Smith, James, used as alias by Tone, 60, 70, 83

Stokes, Whitley, 'The Keeper of the College Lions', 15, 22, 27

Sweetman, John, 134

Talleyrand, Charles, 65, 121, 122

Tallien, Madame, 120

Tandy, James Napper, 'The Tribune', 20, 21, 22, 23, 26, 60, 122

Tate, Colonel, 85

Teeling, Bartholomew, 128

Teeling, Charles G., 52, 103

Tennant, John (United Irishman), 116

Toler, John, 1st Earl of Norbury, 23

Tone, Arthur, brother of TWT, 2, 59, 87, 123

Tone, Francis Rawdon, son of TWT, 40

Tone, Jonathan, uncle of TWT, 12

Tone, Margaret, mother of TWT, 1

Tone, Maria, daughter of TWT, 8, 134

Tone, Mary, sister of TWT, 2, 51, 107

Tone, Matilda, wife of TWT, 7, 14, 15, 79, 82, 86–7, 107–10, 113, 119, 131, 134

Tone, Matthew, brother of TWT, 2, 76, 82, 87, 107, 110, 123, 128, 132

Tone, Peter, father of TWT, 1, 3, 10, 12, 131

Tone, Theobald Wolfe: birth and parentage, 1, education, 2–5; and Mrs Martin, 6, 7; marriage, 8; at Middle Temple, London, 8–11; Irish bar, 12, first pamphlet, 12; second pamphlet, 13; meets Thomas Russell, 14; idyllic summer at Irishtown, 14; founds political club, 15; forms his theory ... to break the connection with England, etc., 17; pamphlet on Catholic cause, 17; visits Belfast, which he calls 'Blefescu', 19–20; founding of society of United Irishmen, 19, description of his person, 21; founding of Dublin club of United Irishmen, 21; approached by Catholic Committee, 24; appointed assistant secretary, 26; visits Belfast again, 27; visits Grattan at Tinnehinch, 28–9; tries for post with Lord Rawdon, 29; journey to Connaught, 30; organises Catholic Convention, 31; secretary to delegation to George III, 32, on Catholic Relief Bill of 1793, 35; and secret committee of House of Lords, 35—6; voted £1,500 and medal by Catholic Committee, 37; attacked by Fitzgibbon, 38; letter to *Faulkner's Dublin Journal,* defending himself, 39; his Kildare cottage, 'Chateau Boue', 41; meets Jackson, 43; compromise with government, 44—5; re-employed by Catholic Committee, 46; seeks post under Fitzwilliam, 47—8; plans to seek French aid to free Ireland, 50; thanked by Catholic Committee, 51; pledges himself on MacArt's fort to continue struggle for independence, 51—2; passage to America, 52—5; views on settlers in America, 56—8; meetings with French Minister in Philadelphia, 55, 59; sails for France under alias 'James Smith', 60; calls on American ambassador in Paris and Minister for Foreign Affairs, 64; meets Nicholas Madgett, 66; meets Carnot, 69; memorials to Directory, 72—5; confers with General Clarke, 72; decides to settle in France, and asks his wife to sail from America to join him, 79—80; meets General Hoche, 81; commissioned chef de brigade, 82; embarks at Brest for Bantry Bay, 85; letter to his wife before departure of fleet, 86—7; account of expedition to Bantry Bay, 92—8; back in Paris, 107; meets Thomas Paine, 109—10; alarmed for his wife's health, 111; re-united with family, 113; at the Texel, 115—17; and death of Hoche,

119; learns of arrest of Leinster Directory, 122; sails for Ireland with Hardy's expedition, 128; arrested and sent to Dublin in irons, 129; trial of, 129—30; last letters to his wife, 131—2; suicide, 132—4; fate of wife and family, 134; assessment of, 135—7

Tone, William, brother of TWT, 2, 9, 10, 110, 123

Tone, William T. W., son and biographer of TWT, 113, 124, 133, 134

'Tribune, The', *see* Tandy, James Napper

Trimleston, Lord, 25

Troy, Dr John T., Archbishop of Dublin, 31

United Irishmen, 19, 21—4, 27, 30, 31, 36, 38, 39, 40, 46, 47, 48, 55, 73, 80, 122, 126, 136

Villaret de Joyeuse, Admiral, 83

'Vintner, The', *see* Byrne, Edward

Wales, Princess of, 42

Walsh, John Edward, 21

Warren, Sir John, 128

Watrin, General, 89, 121

Waudre, Colonel, 94

Wellington, Duke of, 62

Westmoreland, Lord, 46

White, Richard, later Earl of Bantry, 102

William of Orange, 4

Wilson, Thomas, 131, 134

Witherington, Edward, 132

Witherington, Harry, 131

Witherington, Matilda, *see* Tone, Matilda

Wolfe, Arthur, Lord Kilwarden, 44, 133

Wolfe, Theobald, 1, 8

Wolfes of Blackhall, 1, 41

Wood, Captain, 55

Yeats, W. B., 106